BRIGHT NEW YEAR

IVAN COOKE
1889-1981

BRIGHT NEW YEAR

A Centenary Collection of Ivan Cooke's writing

THE WHITE EAGLE PUBLISHING TRUST
NEW LANDS · BREWELLS LANE · LISS · HAMPSHIRE

First published May 1989

With thanks to all who have contributed to the production of this book, and particularly to the artists whose work has given us so much pleasure over the years, whose work is reproduced here: F.E.Swarsbrick ('Swoz'), J. Selwyn Dunn, W. (Bill) Patterson and Rose Elliot. We also thank the Swiss friend of Brother Faithful's who gave generously towards the costs of the book.

© Copyright, Ivan Cooke and The White Eagle Publishing Trust, 1989

British Library Cataloguing in Publication Data
Cooke, Ivan
Bright new year: a centenary collection of Ivan Cooke's writing.
1. Spiritualism
823'.914 [F]

ISBN 0-85487-079-2

Set in 10 on 13 point New Century Schoolbook at The White Eagle Lodge, Liss and London, and printed on Five Seasons recycled paper by Acme Printing Company Ltd Middle St, Portsmouth, Hampshire

Contents

INTRODUCTION 7

THE LADY BRIGHT-NEW-YEAR
Meandering 9
The Lady Bright-New-Year 11
The Man who talked with Flowers 14

CONCERNING WHITE EAGLE
Anniversary 16
Passing of the White Chieftain 18

ANGELUS
The White Eagle Lodge 21
Concerning 'Angelus' 22
Rhapsody 22
The Merchant Ship 23
Little and Good 25
Little and Better 25
Paler but Undaunted 25
Editorial Writhing 25
The Phoenix 26

TWO STORIES
Brother Star-in-his-Heart 27
The Old Lady who strayed into Hell 30

NEW LANDS
The Fairy Hill 33
Lovely Lady 35

STORIES OF TOO-BADE
How to become Superb 38
Motoring into Superbia 39

LONDON IN WARTIME
September Stirrings 43
December 1940 44
What will *you* do 47
The Choristry 47
From 'Evolution' 48

TWO LONGER STORIES
The Mirrored Land 50
The Wedding Ring 55

THOUGHTS ON THE WORK OF THE LODGE
Anniversary 60
Concerning Lighthouses 61
The Grace of God 62

EPILOGUE
Kiss of the Sun 63

Introduction

THIS LITTLE *book is an affectionate tribute to Ivan Cooke, co-founder of the White Eagle Lodge, on the hundredth anniversary of his birth. It is not his true memorial—that is surely in his life's work, which saw the growth of the Lodge, from small beginnings, to a work that touches the lives of thousands of people, in many different parts of the globe. But it is a tribute, to a man whom many who knew him would be happy to call after the title of one of the stories in the volume: 'Brother Star-in-his-Heart'; a man who in his life was unassuming but inwardly dignified, human and not a statue, but with a broad, open heart that surely reflected the light of the spirit, the light of the star, as he did in White Eagle's work.*

At a personal level, I like to remember how moving and inspiring he was as he used White Eagle's words at a meeting or service: but also how, even when doing deeply spiritual work, he was never far from a sense of humour. It was a broad, simple humour that seemed to look round the corner, as it were: to recognise that the real life of the spirit was always larger, more free, than any shape that men on earth could put to it.

Although Ivan Cooke passed into the world of light in 1981, those who continue White Eagle's work are often so strongly aware of him, inspiring them, and, we have to say, bringing the same broad, open heart as he used to bring when on earth. To those who know him that way it is interesting that he usually seems not someone in old age, but has the aura of someone in the prime of life; and perhaps it is true that in this way they are aware of the real Ivan Cooke, his true self. We have never wished to forget this in compiling this anthology. But there is of course also the wish to know something more about his very human personality, to feel understanding of the work he did, and we are sure that there will be many who are pleased to make contact through this collection of writings.

In this short space, we must come now to do what an introduction is supposed to do, and show some of the background to the writings in this anthology. As a writer, Ivan Cooke will be best known to most readers of this booklet for his authorship or editorship of various books based on White Eagle's teaching, such as HEALING BY THE SPIRIT, THE LIGHT IN BRITAIN, *and* THE RETURN OF ARTHUR CONAN DOYLE. *In this booklet, we have wanted to share with readers another side of his writing— the imaginative, creative side. All the pieces printed here are taken from the magazines published by the White Eagle Lodge—the first journal,* ANGELUS, *and the present magazine* STELLA POLARIS, *which superseded it. They were all occasional pieces—stories, editorials and short articles—but in this writing his imaginative side could be more freely expressed; and looking back we find it endearing and inspiring how naturally he was able to write, passing easily from serious things to humorous thoughts (these you will also find included here!). Not only does this bring Ivan Cooke closer, but we are aware that some of the stories and editorials take us very vividly—and often movingly—back to the early years of the White Eagle Lodge, and we hope that readers will enjoy these vivid glimpses too.*

The history of ANGELUS *begins at the same time as that of the White Eagle Lodge—in 1936—and the purpose of the magazine was to be a vehicle for White Eagle's teaching so that this could spread to a wider audience. The third section of this booklet gives in part a little history of its production (with a human dimension to the story!) up to the time of the change to the bimonthly magazine* STELLA POLARIS, *in 1952. Looking back at the early issues, one is aware of just how much creative effort this involved for Ivan Cooke, who as editor often contributed over half the pages for the magazine (which had to appear on the first Sunday of each month) quite apart from attending to its production. As time went on, the editorial and practical burden was partly taken over by others, but one thing we hope this booklet shows is just how creative he was in the writing that was needed to sustain the magazine. In this spirit we have also reproduced one of his paintings, another sphere in which his imagination flowers. The woodcuts and drawings in the text (only the one on page 29 is by Ivan Cooke) are all taken from the printed* ANGELUS *and* STELLA POLARIS.

One friend of White Eagle's from Australia remembers how on a visit to England in 1975 Ivan Cooke, then in his eighty-sixth year, gently took her by the arm and led her happily up the drive to the White Temple, then recently built on the hill at New Lands. We hope that from the writings in this book, readers may feel that they too are led by this warm presence to feel the closeness of a wider, lighter life.

THE LADY BRIGHT-NEW-YEAR

One of the personal qualities Ivan Cooke brought was a feeling of calm steadiness that many people found helped them to relax their mental intensity and look on life with a more easeful, quieter, and more heartfelt vision. We feel this opening piece touches some of this quality. It is an editorial from ANGELUS, *and is followed by the story from which the title of the booklet is taken.*

Meandering

MEANDERING is a blessed word which conjures up memories of wanderings in sunlit meadows, of relaxation, restfulness and a peace such as the world seldom gives but usually steals away. It is a lovely thing to meander whither one will, without a single carking care to hale one back to work and worry. Blessed are those who can meander, and unblessed those who cannot, for they know not what they miss. For there are some people so earnest and intent upon living to the full that—when childhood is past—they leap aboard life as if it were some crowded and swaying omnibus or tramcar, clutch at the nearest strap, and strap-hang for the remainder of their careers; swaying dizzily around corners, grinding in low gear up gradients, shuddering down perilous descents, content to straphang all the way because duty seems to dictate that they straphang. How good and earnest are such people, how stern their devotion, how keen their sense of responsibility to life, how soberly they exist!

More blessed it is to meander—on occasion. Not all the time, of course, for that would steal the zest from meandering—for once in a while, for once monthly, say—? Which brings us to this particular page, which is where the editor is licensed to meander. On this page he goes a-straying (in fancy) to where snowdrops push through a winter's rime of frost, or to a haze of bluebells under greening trees, or to where a great chestnut tree towers up, lit by a thousand white flower-torches—to where white waves are breaking, or little brown birds bursting with song. Occasionally he wonders why drably clad humans do not also burst with song when such miracles of spring are happening. They don't, of course, they cannot sing, alas; strap-hanging does not leave much zest for singing; and when a man or woman reaches this stage the finest tonic and change is a holiday.

But never a strap-hanging sort of holiday—never a holiday crammed in advance with things to be done and seen, so that there is never a moment to spare. These are weariness to the flesh, a torment to the mind, an ache to the spirit. No; we mean a *meandering* holiday full of bird's cries, and quiet wondering and appreciation while sitting under trees, and falling asleep—and thankfulness for being alive, and for the beauty of the earth—thankfulness for all things, and most of all for relaxation—the kind of holiday which carries one along and doesn't have to be carried; not the kind which needs to be strapped up like a heavy travelling bag and lugged everywhere. No, the kind in which one loses oneself as in a dream—when days merge one into the other, and nights are a sweet refreshment, the kind which brings us fulfilment of some deep need and hunger. . . . May such a holiday as this be yours, be mine, this very year; and may it come again next year, and the year after and for ever and a day. For it can come, you know, quite easily—easily, that is, once we learn to meander, and go away *meaning to meander*.

The Lady Bright-New-Year

THIS IS A tale that Father Christmas himself told me one night; and although I cannot vouch for its accuracy, the story has been submitted to a scientific friend of mine, who accepts it in its entirety—that is to say, with the exception of Father Christmas, in whom he does not believe; which is perhaps all the worse for science. So here is the story:—

'In the infinitesimal moment when everything holds its breath and stops—even time itself—' said Father Christmas as he relaxed before my fire. 'When the Old Year dies and everything waits for the coming of the New, the Lady Bright-New-Year descends from on high (from the Sun itself, to be accurate) and alights upon the earth. At that moment she is glorious to look upon—brighter-than-flame, pristine, innocent and virginal—a child of the bright skies. Once she sets foot upon this earth, however, her troubles begin, mainly because she meets and merges with a fellow called Workaday. Or, to put it more plainly, shall we say that the Lady Bright-New-Year actually marries Workaday.

'Now although none of us have actually seen Bright-New-Year vested in her glory, most people have met Workaday—who in his working kit is a grimy and grumpy sort of fellow. These people will say that the two will never make a "go" of marriage; for a child of the sun cannot lightly wed an urchin of the earth. But perhaps they haven't allowed for the beauty and innocence of the bride, or for the fact that even Workaday has his moments as a lover. The sunlight glowed within her and manifested in shining eyes, and golden words, and a bright loving smile; and warm was the loving heart of Bright-New-Year.

'Wedded to such a vision even old Workaday unbended. He could not help but love her in those early days. The two would sit closely before the fire when Workaday's labours ceased at nightfall. Outside January-bite-and-snap raged by, and February-fill-a-dyke soused down. Inside Bright-New-Year would hold forth, while Workaday listened. "I do not understand this darkness upon the earth," she would say. "Nevertheless, soon the Sun will conquer all darkness. No cloud can ever put out the sun. Our Lord the Sun is far mightier than all else. Therefore, the frost and whirling winds only gather because men's hearts are cold with hate." And when February came, she would say: "The skies are weeping only because they grieve over the ways of men. Were it not so they would always be clear and sunlit. Soon,

soon, beloved, skies of happiness shall reign over all the earth. Then the glad New Year which I have brought will change men's hearts. Then all will be well."

'All this while old Workaday would puff away at his pipe, and out of his superior wisdom, smile to himself, thinking that these were only pipe-dreams, winsome and pleasant. He was glad that she didn't have to go out into searing frost or blinding rain to labour. Soon enough she would change her tune. What queer notions she had—in fact, in all she was a queer little thing, but good to love, good to live with—at least while her novelty lasted.

'But came March-bluster-and-blast and the novelty began to wear thin. Workaday felt that now was the time for a bit-of-sense. After all, was it not the duty of every husband to teach his wife this bit-of-sense? And he, Workaday, wasn't going to be lacking in his duty. No, sir; not he! So one night of roaring winds he began. He told her plainly the facts of life. He didn't beat about the bush. Life was real, life was earnest, he said. In fact, life was a tough proposition altogether. Also it was time that she realised that he too was tough, that there were no "notions" about him. Her own pretty fancies were no more than "notions" to the sensible man. They had not reality. They were utterly impractical. What a man wants to get on in the world is a bit of common sense. Because if he didn't look after himself, nobody was going to look after him—not a single soul. In this world business was business, and business was a mysterious something that a chap had either to get on top of or go under. If you got on top everybody liked you. If you didn't nobody had any time for you. That was how things were, and nobody could alter them. Nobody had ever altered them. Nobody ever would alter them. That was how he had always lived, as had his fathers before him. And just look at him, that is if she wanted to see how right he was in all he said and did.

'With that old Workaday tapped out his pipe and wandered off to bed, while poor Bright-New-Year sat tearfully before the fire, and wondered how wrong she had been. For, you see, she was a tender little thing, only three months old at best, whereas the years had graved deep lines upon Workaday, and bowed his back and dimmed his sight. Yet all the same she thought, he must be right because that wise head of his knew so much. Alas for the innocence of her heart, which had led her to entertain 'notions' misleading in the extreme!'

'Then came April, tenderly weeping with sunlight gilding every tear; and she gloried in every flower and sang with every singing bird. During that April even old Workaday renewed his youth. Again they lived, again they loved; and it was then that she conceived her child—O, with such childlike joy, with such deep womanly happiness. "Not I but our son," she said, with laughter and with tears, "shall someday set the world aright."

'This to Workaday was yet another notion; because nothing yet had ever set the world aright, and nothing could or would.

'Despite her happiness, already the world had infused her with itself, tempered her joyousness with its own sadness. She was graver now, more purposeful. Her life she dedicated; she thought, moved, lived within the one orbit, her son-to-be its centre. Even Workaday she kept outside. During those months, she saw her world grow drowsy with summer and later heavy with harvest. She knew then that her Sun was still Lord of Earth—yes, and also life-giver to man.

'She grew heavy with her child. She could no longer wait upon Workaday. With autumn passing, she saw the leaves tremble, whirl, and fall before November's assault. They too were golden with sunlight even as they died. Alas, she herself was longer golden, but gray and lined, weary and drab. Yet golden was her secret hope and shrine within, like a living flame. Then came December, clear and cold, but sunlit. With her the earth had greatly aged, yet it too was making ready, as if awaiting some demonstration, some revelation. The very beasts of the field seemed to sense this too; they would follow her, or watch her passing by wistfully. And then something in her extremity again called forth the manhood in old Workaday, for he too changed, softened and grew tender. Their home, he said, should be made ready, for was not Christmas nearly come? No, no, let her rest by the fire. He would deck that home with holly, richly berried as with drops of blood, and with clinging ivy. He would shake his head, aside, and say, "Poor lass, her time is nearly come. Poor lass, poor lass." Ah, but he hoped that all would go well with her.

'Surely, all went well. For while the Sun trembled beneath the rim of the world her own son was born. Pain and Humility were names borne by the Angels who watched over that birth. After her son was born those two lifted him up and held him high, and named him "Christmas"—Christmas to all the world, Christmas quickening in the hearts of men, Christmas everywhere. So joyous was this time, so wondrous that even the Sun, lying drowsing beneath the horizon, harkened to the bells which rang from every steeple and bestirred itself, and prepared to rise to shine again; and carols of greeting to the Sun were sung by every bird on that glad day.

'What happened afterwards to Bright-New-Year? Why, naturally she became brighter than ever—but not down here. Here she had brought forth, being a daughter of the Sun, a Son of the Sun . . . Even Christmas. This done, Bright-New-Year returned to the Sun for evermore. If you doubt this story look up on any cloudless summer day and you may see her resting upon the bosom of the Sun, bright beyond belief.'

*

Meanwhile, what of Workaday? He doesn't seem to come very well out of all this. Do we know him? If so, a word in season might be helpful. Yes, assuredly we know him. Is he not our neighbour? Does he not strap-hang on our train and perhaps—he lives next door—or maybe, in our own home? It is possible that he may even step into our own shoes on occasion, or wear our clothes, speak, act, think exactly as we do. Why not? Because, you see, the other name of Workaday . . . is Everyman.

Prefacing a later reprinting of this story, Ivan Cooke wrote: 'Many things come to us which are pristine, bright and beautiful—such as, for instance, the innocence of the sky at dawn, the purity of flowers, or of a rainswept sky, or the light within the eyes of a child'—and perhaps in this story he was touching on the difficulty we seem to have in retaining this simple, pure perception in the way we look onto all human life. It was a theme to which he often returned, as in the next piece; an editorial to an early edition of STELLA POLARIS.

The Man who Talked with Flowers

A LONG TIME ago there lived, so they say, a St. Francis of the World of Flowers—a man who so loved flowers that he spoke the language of flowers and understood their wordless speech. Within his heart he heard, and from his heart he spoke. We may be sure of this, for secret things like these are never voiced by the lips or heard by the ears but are for man's secret heart alone.

It is said that this man walked one wintry day in a forest. Beneath his feet the ground was rimed with frost and every twig was jewelled with frost-diamonds; and as he walked he blessed the forest and the ground his feet trod upon; but when at length he rested, wondering at the beauty around him, behold, at his feet a snowdrop had thrust itself up through brown earth and was most sweet to see. Whereupon he knelt beside it, wondering and worshipping that so fragile a flower could be so mighty in purpose as to break through the frozen soil. His heart said softly, 'Snowdrop, tell me of yourself.'

And the flower answered, also within his heart: 'No; you are wrong; I am no longer myself—I am now yourself; for as you see and love me, so do I yield myself and become your flower. There is no need to pluck of even touch me. Already I am wholly yours.'

At that the man answered nothing, absorbing truth as does a flower the sunlight.

'I am your flower now blooming within your own heart. I am become the flower of God thrusting through the frosted soil which imprisons that heart. I am become the promise of God within the heart. See—I am as indomitable as God in my stern courage and will; spring up and live I shall and must despite all adversity and hardship; and none shall stain my purity—none shall sully me.'

'Indeed, you are very pure—bright with purity, I think, ' said the man.

'Now look within. See me as a little light of purity within thee. See me as God within, for I am wholly God's. From me learn to endure, for I have braved all things to become yours.'

Said the man, 'Humbly I accept you, gift from God!'—and bowed himself in prayer.

And after that the flower spoke no more, for everything had been said. But ere the man rose he glanced down, and behold, there was now no snowdrop at his feet! And then he knew his precious flower had become his for evermore.

So said the Snowdrop long ago to the Man who spoke with Flowers. Now is the Season of the Myriad Flowers come. In gardens and in hedgerows across the valleys and in fields and meadows the flowers will blossom and bow with the wind—to the delight of the eye. They can also delight the heart. When they do this deeply then do they enter into that heart, there to abide. This is their message to man.

CONCERNING WHITE EAGLE

The first purpose of the little magazine ANGELUS *was to publish White Eagle's teachings as they were given, to a wider audience. There are now so many friends all over the world for whom White Eagle is a much-loved teacher, who never had the privilege of hearing her speak through Grace Cooke—'Minesta'—that we feel there will be many who will appreciate this description of a public service, from an early* ANGELUS.

ANNIVERSARY.—Although two weeks have passed since our Anniversary, we revert to so wonderful an experience, partly because there are those among our readers who have never entered the Lodge, never even heard White Eagle speak. Had we power of words we would try to picture the Service to these readers, and tell them of the orderly and reverent congregation which filled every seat, the deep silence and sympathy which pervaded the hall.

Blue is the pervading colour at the White Eagle Lodge. The altar is of blue, set against a background of natural (unstained) oak. From above this background a row of shaded blue lighting falls on the plain oaken cross, the lilies and burning candles; while above the lighting is the life-size carving of a white eagle in flight—a graceful and beneficent figure. High on the wall above all is a great silvered symbol representing the cross within the circle.

So much for the scene against which the white figure of White Eagle's medium rises to speak. With this rising a hush falls, and as the address proceeds there comes a profound silence unbroken by cough or movement. The voice of White Eagle is curious in so far as it is neither a man's voice nor a woman's but a blending. There is in it a tenderness and love essentially womanly, and yet both a power and authority. Each word is clear cut and distinct, yet one would never feel that the speaker is of English nationality. The gestures are notable for their grace, ease and fequency. It is said that the Red Indian language consists of but few words, which are largely supplemented by the use of gestures, and this one can well accept after seeing the gestures of White Eagle.

The keynote of the whole is love. Although each address is recorded, those at a distance who read them can form little conception of the power which was their accompaniment, the moving tenderness those printed words once held, the beauty of the whole, the rapt attention and reverence of those who listen. And perhaps our Anniversary Service on February 19th last was the most notable yet held. It stands forth as far more than a preacher and his congregation. The note was too personal, too intimate; rather was it like to that of a father and his family, a word which White Eagle adopted more than once during his address. Yet one gathered that the 'family' incorporated far more than those seated and listening. There were others present, perhaps those who had passed beyond the flesh, and were drawn close again to their loved at this hour; and there was a host still in the body but not in the Hall, and linked to White Eagle and his Lodge by ties of interest and affection. These also he remembered, with these in some subtle way he seemed to speak. . . .

For the first time a microphone was installed, and a record taken of practically the entire service. Until she heard these records White Eagle's medium had never before heard his voice—a strange and notable fact, considering that the two have worked together for some fifteen years. The set of records also forms a most valuable memento of our third Anniversary.

The story overleaf, from the first year of ANGELUS's *publication, is also, we are sure, inspired by the awareness of White Eagle. It shows Ivan Cooke—'Brother Faithful'—responding imaginatively to the American Indian aspect of White Eagle's teaching and presence.*

One of Brother Faithful's pastel drawings of the Isle of Iona

Passing of the White Chieftain

THE SNOW lay thickly on the countryside when the Call came—white upon the prairies, white upon the hills, and the forests garlanded with white. Black was the night, and its breath, rimed with an iron frost which reached even to the stars, and all the night was muted and still when the Call came ringing across its silence.... And no man heard the Call save one.

And he who heard rose, knowing that he must answer, must follow, for the Call, which none may resist, none deny, came ringing through his heart, through all his being. So he rose, and came forth into the night. And upon him and about him was just that robe of the Chieftains with which a chief is clad once only—the robe a Chieftain wears when he goes forth to meet the Great White Spirit, the white robe of ermine, white fox, and squirrel, and he wore his great war-bonnet of eagle's feathers, as a crown, for he was royal; and his hand held his war-bow, and in his belt were both knife and axe.

Thus the White Chief went forth to conquest.

And none of his people heard, none knew; the night encompassed him; and the winds of the night bore him company; and the stars clustered low so that they were set about his war-bonnet and crowned him with starlight and the frost; and the night grew warm to the White Chief, for it knew whither he went and clasped him close.

Long had the Chief waited. Great age sat upon his shoulders, heavy-weighted had been the years; the chief had grown to hunger for the coming of the Call. Long since they had brought home the Chief, his father, and lain his body in the white robe when they took him forth to burial; long since they had taken him, White Chief, as their king and Chieftain. Then had the new chief sent forth a summons to his people—those in the south and east, in west and north, those across the great divide, upon the mountains and the plains, in the forests and the hills; a summons from the White Chief of whom men had yet to learn. For as a deer, so ran he; and no man had cunning in the hunt like his; and his strength was as of three men; and withal, wisdom dwelt on his tongue, and all his thoughts were peace.

At the summons they came, many a brave and chief, to the pow-wow;

they gathered by the firesides of the camp of White Chief and to them he came, the splendour of his youth and manhood as a mantle about him. And spoke with them with tongue of silver and fire; and behold! a dove flew down from the height and settled on his war-bonnet and there he stayed, and none heard the beat of its wings; and a light shone on it, they say, and then it was they knew White Chief as the chosen.

His wisdom was like to moonlight on the waters, the sheen on the snowlands and the heights. The Seven Tribes must dwell as one, he said, in unison, as brethren, and he who drew weapon against his brother they must banish, never to return. Fear and awe silenced them, even the warlike and the fierce; thenceforward the tribes banded as brethren, and none, remembering what they had seen and heard, challenged White Chief.

Ah, long years ago; long years which brought their weariness; one hundred and fifty eight winters had been melted by the spring, the wise men said, since the birth of White Chief—long ago, long, long ago! And the heart grows sad with waiting, and the lines of the years grave themselves deep; and under their weight a man's shoulders would bow, did not steadfastness uphold them.

How long, how long, O Great White Spirit! Hast forgotten thy servant who hearkens for thy calling? The summers burn, the winters blow, but never the Call cometh!

White upon the prairies, white upon the hills, and the forests hUng garlanded with white. All the world held its breath when the Call came; all the night creatures gathered to watch the Chief come forth to answer— and yet of men none woke nor knew . . . none heard.

Swift to answer the Call, swift to obey; for the night grew short, and there was far to go ere dawn—aye, an earth to traverse and her heights to climb. Far to go; and yet a chief may never haste and fret as other men, but quietly go upon his way. He loved his people, chief and brave, squaw and child, dog and horse and beast—all were dear, beloved, beloved. Yet he passed now through their camp with never a backward glance, never a thought, for he who hears the Call hearkens to none other; yet love of all men and all living creatures dwelt in him.

Swiftly across the plains, swiftly over the snow; for age cannot dull nor stay he who obeys the Call—nor shall the miles hinder nor the heights daunt. And the night closed about him as a cloak, and the creatures of the night, beast, bird, furred, feathered and clawed thing, gathered to speed his path. And now the plains fell away and black against the white hills black pine trees held their court, black trees which shouldered the heights.

Now steep are the heights and cold the night, and toilsome the ageing limbs of White Chief; sombre fell the black shadows of the great pines and the wind in them blew shrill and high, as of the lost ones calling to the lost. And bleakness and loneliness would have come upon White Chief but that out of the shadows, out of the mystery, came those bright Ones of the unseen. Plumed and white of raiment they gathered, and their tread was as a thistledown, their voices woven from out of silence. With light upon them they bore him company, chief and brave, woman and child, warriors, and beloved out of a far past, dead, yet endowed with life, afire with life and quickened with love.

They bore him company—by height and defile they accompanied him; and strength ran then in his veins to lift him high over the crags; there was a light within his body, and youth sang in him as he mounted—aye, to where the eagles nested, to the very crest of earthly things, from whence the snow was swept, from whence there shone a little light far away across the plains—the light of his people, of home, of human love.

Long gazed White Chief, and sorrow and gladness sang in his heart—sorrow that he must go, gladness that he had been beloved—ere he turned himself to the last height. Now had the silent Ones left him, so that loneliness spread itself as a pall over the earth, a mighty loneliness encompassed all.

Then came the call closer; as a bird sings to its mate, as a woman to her child, as a flower to the bee which bears to it the mating of a flower—as all of these, and as God reaching out tender hands to gather, so came the Call now, so sweet, so low, so piercing, so entreating, that the life went flowing out of him in answer—as speeds the streamlet to the mighty sea.

So he laid him down to rest; in a tiny cave upon the uttermost height he laid him down, drawing the robe about him until all was seemly, as befits a chief, his weapons beside him. Thus he laid him down, while weariness and age passed out from him, and youth, that was as wine and fire of life, came filling, came flooding to his heart.

Thus was the body of White Chief, White Eagle of the Seven Nations, laid down to death; but the heart of him, tender and great with compassion to all, the soul of him, his spirit, pure and high, rose up.... Arose, to see the dawn break over a world transfigured, enwrapt with beauty; to see the dawn, mystical and holy, the dawn beautific.... Arose, and thus went forth to God.

ANGELUS

We would now in this anthology like to print a few extracts from editorials and asides when Ivan Cooke was writing about the magazine ANGELUS *itself—its purpose and its production. These are both serious and humorous. The first is the opening editorial of the first issue of* ANGELUS *(June 1936), describing its purpose. We still find this a deeply inspiring description of the White Eagle work as a whole.*

THE WHITE EAGLE LODGE.—The White Eagle Lodge came into being because it stands primarily for Unity, and embraces in its teaching many a school of thought. While embodying the teaching of Theosophy, Christian and Spiritual Science, New Thought and Spiritualism, it would follow and advocate all paths which lead to Truth. Thus the White Eagle Lodge holds to no creed save unity with all, no other aim save Brotherhood. The name chosen for the Lodge is designed not for the enhancement of any one individual, incarnate or discarnate, but as representative of a school or aspect of thought which might be symbolised by the White Eagle—the bird of vision, of soaring wings and sunlit skies. In this connection it may be well to recall that the symbol of an eagle has always represented the mystical aspect of Christianity as embodied in the Forth Gospel of St. John.

If it be loyal to it self, the Lodge should seek to be a mystical Church of the Spirit, its mission to send forth such truth as has been entrusted to it; to hold nothing to itself, but ever seek to give; to place service before numbers, power, or popularity in a world where service is desperately needed. Such a Church is fulfilling itself if some who are lonely can find in it companionship and affection; if some who have lost faith can find a stable resting place again; and the sick in mind or body can gain from its healing the health of soul and body they lack.

So much for the ideal behind the White Eagle Lodge. May this journal prove itself to be a part and portion of this putting forth, setting forth of such truth. . . .

On the other side of the picture, there was the practical business of producing and duplicating ANGELUS *monthly. As described more fully in the introduction, the first volumes of* ANGELUS *were typewritten and then duplicated on a hand-turned machine that tried the patience even of Brother Faithful—not to mention his family. The next three extracts show some editorial letting-off steam at this process, and 'The Merchant Ship' shows pride over the first printed edition of* ANGELUS *(December 1939), which, with its engravings and woodcuts, is still a delight to look at.*

CONCERNING 'ANGELUS'.—The first issue of ANGELUS has been kindly received. Its readers have overlooked shortcomings, praised any merits, and translated their kindliness into action by either passing on their own copy, or obtaining further copies for their friends. ANGELUS and its staff anticipated no less, for we grow to expect kindness from members and friends, since many kindly people come this way. But we thank you, one and all.

Do not, however, enquire of the Editorial staff (comprising one person) why the first issue of ANGELUS was duplicated and not printed. Do not stress the many advantages of printing over duplicating. The staff will only respond with a pallid smile. It knows the answer. Do not repeat your question in our duplicating, binding, and despatching Works (the Works measuring six feet by eight, and staffed by two persons). They have turned the handle of the duplicator some thousands of times—sorted, arranged and bound so many thousand sheets! They know, also,—none better. Why rouse them to frenzy, or send them into a decline?

Nevertheless, ANGELUS, made beautiful and more perfect, will, in due course, go out into the world in printed form, and thus carry its message to the many instead of the few.

RHAPSODY
By the Editorial Staff

Behold, out of an overhead fog the rain descendeth on greasy pavements
   And all the air is stiff with damp; nevertheless
   Spring is here; although you wouldn't think it!
   Notice! old gentlemen take fat dogs for jauntier walks
   In Kensington; as well they might, for there is no jauntier place
   In February. O, to be in Kensington now that February's here!

   Tell me, my printers of Angelus, is the February number complete?
   Complete! Allah be praised! Has the duplicator turned
   Those many thousand times while pages gush forth?
   Has the duplicator broken thrice and no more?
   Praise be to goodness! Ink lies upon your brows, O staff;

Inked is your raiment, and all the air was blue. Nevertheless,
Thank goodness!

Have you addressed *all* the blessed envelopes—
(Including that plain one to the lady who doesn't want it known?)
Inserted all the copies of Angelus, stamped all, and posted them?
Praise be! Hard is this to realise—that our journal is written,
Duplicated, pages counted, bound, posted—that all the labours
Of the month are over. Rest then, my staff; lay down
Your toilworn bodies. See, spring cometh, and all the earth is glad!
Take your ease under this blissful fog; go forth, make holiday.
Any policeman will guide you to the park or else to the British Museum
Where you may be joyful;
Thou hast laboured long—
Go forth; Kensington applauds you, and countless readers will (perhaps)
Launch countless blessings . . . Go forth, go forth. . . .

But stay—stay—stay! Just one small moment!
We have forgotten. . . . What about—
The Angelus for *March*! ! ! . . . Come, take out the duplicator again,
Bestir yourself, get busy. . . . Let's get down to it once more.

THE MERCHANT SHIP.—Some few years ago a firm of merchants thought to themselves, 'Our warehouses are filled with goods which we believe could be traded at great profit, both to our customers and to ourselves. No one except ourselves knows how valuable are these goods. So busy are men with their own affairs that they will not listen. If those same goods remain in the warehouses they will be wasted. Yet a multitude hunger. What can we do?'

After long thought they decided that they would build a ship, the hold of which could be stored with their goods. Then their ship could sail the seas, putting into many harbours, finding many customers. So they set to work to build, although they possessed little experience of shipbuilding. And those wise in the ways of the sea told them that their ship would surely founder in some storm, 'For,' they said, 'we have seen many another enterprise of this sort, and most fail.'

Nevertheless the ship was built, albeit somewhat clumsily, and when completed some laughed at her, saying that they doubted if she would prove watertight with a hull so ungraceful and planking so clumsy. Yet, when launched, the ship sailed bravely forth, lying closely to the wind, and staunchly withstanding the storms. She sailed the seas, and little by little many a trader heard of the goods she carried, so that at length she traded with the Indies, the Americas, and many another country.

The merchants grew to scan the horizon against her coming; for she bore sails blue as the deep of the seas, and her masts and spars and tackle were of silver glistening in the sunlight. And after each month she would return to port to have her holds refilled with the goods stored within those warehouses. Infinite pains were taken that none but the best should go forth.

With the result that each month the numbers of those who traded with the ship grew larger, until at length there came a time when the holds of the ship could no longer contain all the goods demanded. Then again the builders of the ship took thought, deciding that it was obvious that another and larger ship was required, and moreover, that she must be built with more grace, become more worthy to carry their goods. So they hied them to a builder of ships, and for a certain price—somewhat of a breathtaking price—they ordered another ship, swift and graceful and seaworthy. And for the first voyage the merchants have crammed her holds with better wares than ever before (so they think).

And.... This is the first voyage of that second ship; she has sailed forth with sails of blue, and spars silver as the dawn. And.... the name of that ship is.... 'Angelus.' She has sailed across the seas of time and space to *you*. May she find safe anchorage, and her goods a welcome... with you.

The very human aspect of Brother Faithful's approach to his work also comes out in these following extracts which open our eyes to just some of the practical difficulties of keeping a monthly magazine in print during wartime. In the first extract it is the compulsory restrictions on all journals, due to paper shortages, that are being explained.

[*May 1942*] LITTLE AND GOOD.—The fiat has gone forth. The powers that be have decreed that all journals must be again reduced. So ANGELUS this month appears in its new garb. It should be noted that these restrictions concern the amount of paper only, and not the contents of a journal. Our readers will therefore find, we hope, that the new ANGELUS contains as much reading matter as before, even if that matter is compressed into a smaller space.

[*June 1942*] LITTLE AND BETTER.—On the whole, and not altogether to our surprise, the new and smaller ANGELUS (smaller in size, not in contents, by the way) seems more popular than the old. For one thing, it is likely to travel through the post in better shape; for another, it fits the pocket or handbag; and for another, it is susceptible to still further improvement—as will be seen in due course. In the June issue we are reverting to our woodcuts, for so long a feature of ANGELUS, and hope that a new series of 'Tree' woodcuts will be available by then. By July we hope to produce an improved cover design.

[*October 1942*] PALER BUT UNDAUNTED.—In a few months' time our blue cover paper for ANGELUS will be exhausted. It can't be helped, unfortunately; supplies have given out, at least for the duration. Our printer's remaining stock of blue cover-paper has been reserved to bind our second book of Spiritual Unfoldment, which we plan and hope will be ready for its readers by Christmas—but about which date our printer seems to have some doubts. In the meantime, we shall choose the best cover material at present available for ANGELUS. . . .

[*October 1942*] EDITORIAL WRITHING.—Just between ourselves, the editorial soul writhes at paper restrictions. It doesn't like the thinner paper, the smaller type. It would have ANGELUS wholly beautiful. It longs for the day when it will be able, so to speak, to spread itself on rich cream laid paper. But it just can't do anything . . . and millions of other people are in the same state of mind. So it is not to be wondered at if other people get a trifle brusque and snappy, nor should we feel unduly hurt. They don't mean it, bless them; it's only the strain of things.

What causes the strain? Again, just between ourselves, isn't it because most people are frightened—frightened as regards their personal affairs, their dear ones, frightened at cruelty and horror on a world scale? That is why they sometimes seem unduly harsh and lacking in understanding. A frightened man is an unreasonable man, often an impolite and harsh man . . . And yet he needs sympathy, patience, even compassion—because the frightened are always pitiful.

These are the home truths the editor tells his editorial soul when it writhes unduly, when it gets hot under the editorial collar.

In December 1951, after fifteen years of Ivan Cooke's editorship and careful nurturing, ANGELUS *was brought to a close, and the new bi-monthly magazine,* STELLA POLARIS, *was launched. This was a change that seemed in keeping with the growth and developement of the work, and the idea of the new magazine, and its title, were given White Eagle's blessing. The following piece is Brother Faithful's opening editorial to the new magazine.*

THE PHOENIX.—The phoenix, according to Oriental mythology, was a bird which having lived for five hundred years, then built itself a heap of sticks. This done, the fire was lighted and the indomitable bird sat itself down upon that pyre and was utterly consumed. But not finished: a notable feature about a phoenix is that it arises after its fiery sacrifice of itself, rejuvenated, renewed, purged and purified, eager for higher, wider flights into the heavens. Can any parallel be drawn between the phoenix and the Angelus we all feel a little wistful about at the moment—especially the editor, to whom Angelus has seemed like a child these fifteen years past? Why not? True, Angelus has not been in existence for quite five centuries (although on occasion during the war it seemed so to the editor). Neither has Angelus met its end in quite so spectacular a manner as the phoenix, its disappearance being rather a fading out than a burning out. But in its capacity for resurrection, for arising renewed, reborn, re-created; for becoming stronger, finer, purer, wiser—well, here Stella Polaris yields place to the phoenix. But if Stella Polaris does not surpass Angelus, then is our effort vain.

So the first Christmas Stella Polaris comes to you, with sixteen extra pages, in larger, clearer type, and with a new cover, seeking your approval—and finding, I hope, your welcome and friendship.

TWO STORIES

In this section we print two 'Little Tales of the Spirit' from ANGELUS. *The first of these two fables, we are sure, echoes Ivan Cooke's complete absorption in the work of the White Eagle Brotherhood.*

Brother Star-in-his-Heart

ONE NIGHT long ago a man journeyed forth from the places of men, across the desert lands. A hunger for that which he knew not held him, so that for long his toil for gold and self had become arid as desert dust. Body had wearied of things of the body, mind and heart ached with emptiness. That night not a soul save he walked beneath the stars, and the night breeze touched him softly, softly, as if the arms of the night caressed; and the dew of night fell like the kiss of a flower upon his bared brow.

Against this wondrous night hung a star, clear, pure, bright—so softly luminous that it seemed drawn close to earth; and this he watched, with dulled eyes of weariness; and to his sick fancy it seemed the star moved before him and he followed until at last he saw it crowning a high hill as if at rest thereon. Forthwith he climbed to follow.... This was a stern man, strong and ruthless in the world, and that same will which had torn from other men abundance for himself, spurred wearying body higher and higher still until at last he neared the summit.

The star still shone there—still gleamed, miracle of miracles, near to his hand, still white and pure, still without stain although it was held by earth. Now came there fear upon him, a craven trembling in limb, a wilting even in the heart. Yet that indomitable will prevailed, and he laid hands upon the star, stooped and raised it, albeit he had to turn his eyes from its flame. To his touch it was clear and cool, as if wet by heavenly streams, and yet tremulous with life. Life breathed within it, and life it radiated; yet despite its light and life it had become a tiny thing, no larger than a jewel of purest sheen, this gem from heaven's mine.

The man wrapped it in a kerchief, and hid it in a secret pouch against his breast, together with gold and other jewels he carried for barter—how dull those jewels now—and took his way back again to the ways of men, through a dawn of pearl, delicate as white innocence. Within the city he saw men's faces now as stern and hard, unutterably empty of light, so that a great pity came upon him, and from out of that pocket he gave them gold and jewels until they clustered round joyfully, yet wondering at his madness. The secret star he gave not away, but felt it warm and clear shining into him, as if his body were the body of night itself and it a star lighting his blackness. Having emptied his pouch, he went home to where he kept a secret store, took more gold, more jewels, and gave again, and yet again until all he possessed was gone, and he a man of wealth stood penniless.

Yet was the madness still upon him, and the star now become disquieted as if itself urgent to fly away. He feared no thing so much as this, so drawing away from the crowds again feasted his eyes upon its wonder, and then wrapped it tenderly again and hid it beneath the steel and leather helm upon his head. And now the star lay quietly luminous and shining as if at rest; and strangely his thoughts become no longer dull and earthly but shining and starlike also, as if they were become as down and plumage on some winged wisdom, the sweep of which swept ignorance away. For now with widened vision saw he all things. The page of truth lay bared, the tree of life gave of its fruit; he was become all wise, and saw as God seeth the soul of all creation. He saw no longer barren fields and plains scarred by battle and rapine, drabness and shadowing death; no longer men diseased and crippled, men hating each other, ignorant of all things, but men as gods wise and poised and wholly beautiful. Man made perfect—that and no other was the Ultimate Thought of God, and this the Plan towards which Creation laboured and travailed, this the consummation for which all sorrow and all suffering paid the price. Splendid, pure and beautiful he saw an earth stripped of earthliness. With shining mind grown luminous he went forth to tell men this wondrous thing, this truth and hope surpassing.

They clustered close to listen. What, was no more gold forthcoming, they asked. Naught but this torrent of words, this uncanny transfigured look that struck fear into them. To fear was to hate, to hate destroy. Men destroy with anger that gives edge to destruction. One flung a stone, one struck him, then more stones and blows, and so they beat him down—down—down—and leering left him.... And then with feeble hands he reached and found the Star. No other thing had he; this they could not see, for their eyes were held. With dying hands he touched that quivering life and placed it near his heart and then fell back. Then dying heart and living star beat together, and into heart crept a light beyond and above that known on land or sea. He loved—with heart grown like a star he loved—and never had he known love such as this before, not even when mind held all wisdom. No need to forgive, naught to forgive those who had slain him. Them he loved also.

And thus he died that death which opens the shining gate to life, this first of the Brethren of the Star. A mythical tale? A legend of long ago? Listen! It happened but yesterday! It happens this very day; it will happen again tomorrow. For there are those who wander seeking they know not what, and by dint of climbing high above the earth can find the Star. Then do they cast away worldliness—it has no longer value; then find they the wisdom which reveals all things—which points to sacrifice. Sacrifice proves love. Whereupon self dies, and the soul forgiving all, loves all things.

In their hearts a Star! A Star within their hearts, won and worn by selflessness, a Star that is the Brother's shrine and sacrament.

This Star, Brethren, is that which led the Wise Men to find Christ. You, Brethren, should know each other by the Star within; for in Star-light Christ was born to the heart of man long ago; is born today; and will be born throughout the generations of men.... On Christ-Mass Day.

The Old Lady who Strayed into Hell

A truish tale for goodish people

... THE LAND of hell is not ugly, as supposed; on the contrary, it has a rare beauty. Nature's changing seasons mirror an ever-unfolding pageantry, perhaps of winter clad in greys and whites, or a springtide of tender greens and blossoms; then later comes summer, rich, gracious, motherly; and then autumn, hale and full of the bounty of harvest. No, beauty is writ across nature, even in hell, beauty without scar or blemish. But the inhabitants of hell don't pattern their lives on beauty; they don't hesitate to despoil her by the erection of squalid houses, lined out in streets and squares with the smallest possible spot of land for the ugliest possible house, all getting daily and nightly grimier and dingier from a pall of grime that overhangs the towns.

Grime, mark you, that permeates the people's homes, their minds, their hearts. Perhaps that is why the people in hell find it so difficult to be kind. Being otherwise, they have fears, one of the other, each thinking his fellow likely to slander or despoil him; (indeed, many go hungry or workless). Being fearful they seek protection one from the other, and even band one against the other in communities or nations, each intensely apprehensive. Then they need ever greater armies to safeguard (so they think) one nation from the other, and suspicions and fears multiply until at last war comes, and these unfortunates are decimated. Or else, if someone saves the nations from war, they call him traitor or coward, and say honour demanded war.

Which is all very sad and illogical. But then, this is hell, you see, where folk are not so very rational—as yet. And being hell, it makes the story of the old woman who was kind far more notable than otherwise. Not that they thought kindness anything extraordinary. They took it in their stride, more or less. Some people said that she was kind because she just couldn't help it.

Others said 'How easy it is for *her*. Comes natural-like, you see.'

And others, 'Yes, you see, she was born that way. Can't imagine her different. But she's a little *peculiar,* you know.'

And so our old lady just went on being kind in a natural kind of way because she just liked people, because she saw something likeable in the most unlikely; and liking them, she was interested. And each soul instinctively reacts to another's interest; it needs only interest to awaken, to quicken, to gain interest in response.

To the old lady her next-door neighbour, her milkman, the grocer, the beggar, the girl at the Post Office, the errand boy—all were *living people*. Because they were living, instead of automatons, she just couldn't help talking. And it was not in what she said, not even in those bright old eyes full of humanity and humour, nor in heartening counsel of hope and courage—not alone in these, but in some pervasive and persuasive *essence* which was herself.

People were interesting. So she said, so she proved. Yes, even that soured lady behind the counter at the Post Office, who chilled hundreds of customers daily. It was only a matter of routine, you see, for the old lady; she was interested, so she talked, and gradually the spinster thawed, told of a wartime bereavement, of parents to be helped, of her bodily ailments, handicaps and frustrations. All the while the little old lady listened in a way that continually drew forth and gave in return sympathy, counsel, pointers towards courage and hope. She had a way with her, had the old lady, a way which carried her onward through life, bright eyed and healthy, hearty and happy, and brought her at last to a peaceful end. People said then—So she's gone. Dear, dear, dear! I'm sorry. Hopelessly unpractical, you know, and a little *peculiar* ... but—but ... I'm sorry. I think we must send something, or perhaps *I'll* go to the funeral' .... And so many actually sent flowers, or went themselves that no one would have been more surprised than the little old lady, if she had known.

But perhaps she did. Anyway, at the time of her funeral (or thereabouts, for there is no time up there) she was seated on a grassy bank talking to an Angel, somewhere in heaven. And there is no doubt that she was interested; for the Angel was saying earnestly, 'Cannot you hear heaven's welcome, good and faithful one? Here, all is responsive to love, to kindness; all that you have given forth, all the treasure of your heart can here be made manifest in a pulsating light and beauty beyond mortal dreams.'

'Thank ye' said the old lady 'but I'm not stopping.'

'Listen!' pleaded the Angel, 'and you will hear the welcome of the heavenly host. Listen! the silver trumpets peal, and yearning hearts long to thank you for your kindliness to some loved one still below.'

'Hark ye also, young man!' said the old lady, 'Listen with your heart, like I'm doing. Hear ye nothing?'

'I hear a cry of fear and pain.'

'That's *them*!' cried the old lady. 'Poor dears, they don't know no better than to cry and hate and hurt. But heaven's not heaven to me when I can hear them. I've got to go back, young man.'

'But here is joy, a deep deep draught of ecstasy. Here, in this fair land, the Master walks, and you may touch His robe and feel His hand upon your heart. Stay, weary one!'

'Bless you, I know *that* Master, and He knows me. His hand knocked at my door one night. He has entered and supped with me, and His heart also hears the cry. No, I'll not be staying, thank ye. I know the road.'

'But the road is hard to travel; full of the pangs of birth, for through the gateway of human birth must you go, to feel again the weight of the flesh, the sorrows of your kind.'

'But they've been so very good to me, the people down there. I can't forget, you see. I've got to help some more.'

'You choose to go—you choose hell instead of heaven?'

'I choose to help, young man, as you know in your heart that I should. You think I didn't know your heart as you mine? Me and you, we're close—though far apart lie our ways. God be with ye!' And she turned away.

The Angel stood upon the heights, tall and gracious, and filled with light; and watched the old lady take the long path—watched her form dwindle and darken and fade in the mists; and in his heart sang praise and joy, deep, exquisite, ecstatic; yet full and keen with pain.

NEW LANDS

In contrast to the two preceding ones, the next two pieces were written later, for STELLA POLARIS. *The article, 'The Fairy Hill', recounts (in 1966) the preparation of the country home of White Eagle's work at New Lands—a wonderful step forward in the unfolding of the work. The other piece is more general but 'Lovely Lady' describes, and always makes us think of, the beech trees in New Lands garden.*

The Fairy Hill

IN IRELAND, should a hillock stand near a cottage, that hillock is usually called a fairy 'lysse'; meaning a place where the little people must be left undisturbed, and treated respectfully, or else they might do mischief. Here in Hampshire we have of course our own 'lysse', or 'Liss', a village from which a hill slopes gently up to where New Lands stands near its crest. Not that the villagers down in Liss take much account of fairies—they know better, being 'Hampshire'. That's what comes of living in a valley.

Twenty-one years ago, when the daffodils were nearly over, and when cold springtime winds were blowing, a man (myself) worked in the garden at New Lands, scything away at its lawn, where grass stood knee-deep—scything because there was no one else to do it, most able-bodied men having been caught up in the war, then drawing to its close. In that year, 1945, nearly everything else had drawn to a close—food and clothing and human happiness were all giving out under the strain.

Yet all the same that man scything felt as happy as ever he had done in all his days. While the cold wind blew and he wiped the sweat from his brow he felt just happy—happy because he felt there was a miracle in the sweetness of it all; in the scent of cut grasses, the feeling of the countryside, in the sight of the rolling downs, in the feel of soil beneath the feet, in the sound, swing and slice of the scythe—in all, was blessing and sweetness bestowed.

Because, you see, this was indeed a piece of fairyland in which he worked, with nearby a hilltop abandoned to the fairies to become their very own 'lysse'—and who can say fairer than that? It didn't seem to matter much if that big house in the midst of it all had been a war-time nursing home, and had subsequently been taken over by evacuees who had flitted away leaving the house disconsolate; it didn't matter if there wasn't a garden implement in the place fit to use; or that weeds galore were bursting through each garden path, that the kitchen garden was cramped up with weeds, and the orchard had been overrun. After all, three or four acres of derelict garden and orchard could be tackled. Yes—even while away beyond the gardens waited another twenty-four acres of fields impoverished by war-time cropping. A gardener's cottage, complete with huge, rusty iron kitchener and minus all modern conveniences, even a bath; a stable and coach house; a derelict cowshed and pigsties overgrown with nettles up to six feet high—all these were waiting. But withal New Lands was a lovely place, full of promise.

This was *New Lands*, new lands of promise opening; and here White Eagle had directed his family, first describing it so exactly that the house and gardens had been recognised at first sight and the family had immediately opened negotiations for its purchase, mostly on a basis of faith-in-hand (and no money to speak of). Though the purchase became delayed by someone offering the owner much more than his selling price, all went well subsequently and the property, lock (few door-locks that worked), stock (no stock anywhere) and barrel (no barrels) became the property of Mrs. Grace Cooke*, with only a mortgage interest amounting to one pound daily to hinder her enjoyment, this same interest payment entailing a considerable yearly loss during the next few years.

What fun it was to get down to the job, and by degrees to 'get the property up together'—to use a Hampshire phrase. Of course, the fairies must have done most of it by the waving of their wands. The rest was just hard work. But hard work brings results. That, and the generosity of kind-hearted people has since lifted a burden of debt off New Lands, so that now it stands well cared for, house and gardens and fields alike, with four neat cottages replacing the derelict stables, cow houses, gardener's cottage and pigsties, and behind, inspiring the fairies and the other folk who have worked to this end, always the power and influence of the Spirit. . . .

[*The story continues, prophetically:*]

What then of the future? One can only see continued expansion, which must come soon now for the chapel, the office and the book-storage accommodation is all becoming outgrown. But expansion must come quietly, gently, purposefully, and never ruthlessly or dominated by the worldly-minded; because the fairies abiding on and within the 'lysse' or the fairy hill mustn't be disturbed or frightened.

And yet, beyond all talk of fairies we know that long ago Brethren of the Light dwelt on the hill at New Lands, and that the essence of their gentle lives still abides. It is this which calls; so that some day on the hill another temple must arise to continue their work for the blessing of men and of the little people nearby. May it not be too long in its arising, and may it be filled with power and blessing to enrich the lives of men.

In 1967 New Lands was made over to the Trust of the White Eagle Lodge.

Lovely Lady

SHOULD YOU and I meet outside the garden doorway to the New Lands chapel, we might decide to stroll down to the Monks' Walk. The way would pass between awakening rose trees, newly pruned, and past the lily pond until we came to the stone steps leading down to the Monks' Walk. Here we might halt, gazing down the valley for a moment, and on our right, not twenty yards distant, we would see our Lovely Lady. Not that we would see her beauty all at once; because mostly our eyes are unseeing, and so dull of response that our reaction when seeing our Lovely Lady is that she looks like many another English beech tree, albeit standing staighter and more graceful than most.

Lovely Lady, so we are told, was planted as a seedling about eighty or even a hundred years ago, part of a beech hedge perhaps, which would account for the row of fully-grown beech trees which today edges the New Lands garden; the straightest and most seemly of all of them being our Lovely Lady herself, who stands half as tall again as New Lands itself.

We have yet to look upon her with opening eyes, with seeing vision. Her topmost twigs reach towards the sky with a wondrous delicacy and sensitivity, responsive to every breath of wind, yet each bough and limb beneath giving reinforcing strength against stress or storm. No mortal architect could plan with matching grace or beauty, nor could his ideas fit into the landscape in this fashion.

Now in this gentle February sunshine let us seat ourselves on one of her roots, and look; rummaging in crevices of those roots I have brought out two tiny skeleton leaves, relics of last year's crop. Here, one on each hand they lie, by a miracle unbroken, unsoiled. 'In little things' is it not said, 'In tiny fragile things, the Lord cometh; and on fragile things (such as the human soul) the Lord worketh.' Here in our hand lie evidences of His toil and care. For of the ten or twenty thousand leaves which last year clothed Lovely Lady, no two leaves would be identical in design or shape. . . .

Now we let those two tiny leaves flutter away. Down they go into the rusty winter grass; soon perhaps they will be dispersed, absorbed altogether in rich mould at the tree's root. They which formerly spoke of death are transformed, transmuted into new life, whose promise is already in the tree. Do you doubt it? Feel then these swelling leaf buds; feel how they are alive with the promise of coming spring, with new thrusting energy flooding through every fibre of our Lovely Lady's being. What seemed like death to her has taken the semblance of life recurrent, of life eternal. From dust of earth spring up eternal verities. When we let those two skeleton leaves flutter down we identified ourselves with the eternal rhythm which encradles all creation, with that rhythm which bears all creation along with it, ordaining for each creature its birth in time and place, the promise of growth into fulfilment, each in its measure, and then a resting period and transient death which is its own fulfilment; followed by renewal.

Our earth and all that moves thereon follow the same sequence. Our leaf might well be likened to an earth, or to a star sequence, far flung beyond man's power of apprehension, in space beyond his seeing, in magnitude beyond his imagination. Birth and then growth and fulfilling, completing by what man thinks to be death, is the whole sequence of creation. But always is death followed by new and finer life.

This applies to us ourselves as well, to those inner selves of ours of which we are hardly aware, those more tender selves we hide away from sight. These too will endure beyond death.

Men say that in spring the sap rises to reclothe bushes or trees with new foliage. But trees are ministered to by mightier Agents—by Sunlight and by Air, by Water and by Earth; from all of these—from Fire and Air, Water and Earth—does Lovely Lady take, and shapes her form and weaves her raiment, decorous and subdued in winter, gay and splendid in due season.

Now the future opens to our vision, revealing not only her outer daily life, but also her inner secrets and her purpose. Now springtime has quickened and renewed her. No longer stark and naked, she stands forth robed in tender green, her own incomparable green, beechy-green, behind which veil, and screened by it, all manner of matchings and lovemakings by little harmless creatures are taking place. Generations of bird life have been sheltered by our tree, and for generations the little furred animals have sought and found haven behind her greenness. This our tree has herself always grown in sancuary; she has never known poisonous sprays, nor yet use of artificial fertilisers to sour the soil around her roots, and little creatures have always found safety and shelter among her branches and roots.

Shelter—that is their mother tree's main concern for them; so with the onset of summer she sheathes herself in darkening foliage where her little creatures can better hide while pursuing their nest-building, the hatching and feeding of their young, sheltered from all harm; for scores of years Lovely Lady has been mothering countless creatures of the air and of the woodlands and hedgerows, and spending herself to beautify our earth.

She stands and lives in sanctuary because daily and all the year through prayers go out from the New Lands chapel for the healing of the sick, and for the healing of the sick and angry nations of the world. And all such prayers reach out to all lands around New Lands, serving to shield them from the harshness of an outside world. Is this why and whence Lovely Lady has inherited her loveliness, the crowning and fulfilment of which is soon to come? For now in vision we see autumn returning to us, now have all these birds and beasts hatched and sheltered in our tree scattered and dispersed. Now tribute has to be made to our tree by those powers whom she has served, the winds and waters of the earth and sunlight from the heavens; they will come to deck her, do her homage. For a day comes when she will be clothed with the sun, robed in autumn sunlight; we shall see her with golden autumn sun-kissed leaves shot through by crimson. Royally robed shall she stand, and perhaps those innocent creatures whose lives and well-being she has fostered, will come back to pay her tribute. Wild and free as they deem themselves, still they have made their link with our tree. So robed with sunlight she stands proudly, well knowing this robe she wears is the robe of her renunciation; for soon all will be taken away. One day we shall see her golden robe has fallen gently down to lie around her feet, like a carpet of gold, fast sinking into earth. Soon will she stand bared and alone against the coming winter; more gracious and graceful then in all her royalty. Against the winter skies she will stand, and still her branches will reach heavenward as in prayer. They symbolise her nature, for all her life has been a giving of herself to help and beautify the earth, and all her years have brought a fragrance to mankind.

STORIES OF TOO-BADE

One popular series of stories Ivan Cooke wrote for STELLA POLARIS *was based on the opinions of a little Pekinese dog of his acquaintance—each one signed 'Too-Bade the Peke'—as were the two following pieces. May the first one encourage us all to be upright and confident in bearing!*

How to become Superb

PARDON ME if I give you a little advice: you see, we *Pekes* have a reason for any display *we* may choose to make, because our ancestors specialised in display, so much so that their mien and bearing put even the Emperors they served into the shade. Indeed, few bothered to look at an Emperor when a bevy of royal dogs was in attendance, clad in a regalia which not only enhanced their natural beauty but made them positively superb to behold—superb, that is, in gait and bearing and the regal condescension that graced them.

Are these qualities likely to abate in the course of a thousand or so years? Certainly not. Providence still places us only in the very best homes because only *we* can adorn those homes. Hence our pride does not abate. On the contrary; it comes out in all we do. Who else, for instance, possesses a tail such as ours, a burgeoning plume with a delicate curl or wave, carried high over the back? Who else possesses so stiff a spine so arrogantly carried? Where else will you find legs comparable with ours—legs which are themselves heavily plumed (as a rude person once said 'looking like sailor-trousers')—forelegs which when we walk are flung out with what any other dog might call a 'preposterous flourish,' but in *us* is right and seemly?

In short, humans, where will you find our like? Nowhere! Then why, O preposterous humans, do you not take example by what you see? For instance, you expect us to take you, safely on the end of your lead, for a daily walk. We do this out of the kindness of our heart. We stalk ahead, tail plumed and waving, head arrogant in all it surveys, spine bristling with pride, forelegs (heavily sailor-trousered!) flung wide in a superb march. What about yourselves, humans? Do you catch the infection of a just pride from your companion and patron? Not a bit of it. Your draggle-tailed walk is positively lamentable. Your legs, let it be said, are not flung wide, nor would the wearing of sailor-trousers grace them. Instead of a tail like a plume, you drag a dismal umbrella after you, while your head droops and your eyes are fixed on the gutter.

And this happens, poor dear humans, with such an example ever before you! Have you no pride of gait or bearing? Apparently not. Let us then confer, in order to seek the reason for this lamentable droopiness. 'What's bred in the bone comes out in the bearing' is a saying of us Pekes. In other words, *it's character that does it!*. It's our character which bestows our walk and bearing on us. Having something to be proud about we're naturally proud. What about you? Haven't you got something? Yes, yes, surely you have... a delightful companion who takes you out daily on your lead. Come now—lift your eyes from the gutter; straighten your shoulders, fling away that umbrella—unless of course you want to shelter us from the rain—spurn it, I say! Throw out your chest, lift your head high, taking care not to tread upon a superior person at your feet, walk with a wide-flung swagger. Do this, and your character will be coming out as it should; do this, dear humans, to show that you profit by *our* example—which we expect (as a matter of course) to be kept specially well-groomed and well-fed during this period of instruction; so that eventually when we both walk out together as equals, both well-primed with pride, we shall assail the beholder with a surpassing wonder because we are... well, just superb!

(Signed): TOO-BADE THE PEKE.

Motoring into Superbia!

IF YOU could come for a ride in our car (indeed, *my* car) it would be pleasant indeed. Unfortunately, however, there is no room for Humans other than my Two, one of whom drives and the other constantly watches for other assassin motor cars hurling themselves up on our left-hand side, while the driver dodges attacks from every other quarter. I am safely seated between the Two on my special cushion; an admirable arrangement.

I have always regarded this art of spreading myself properly as a major acquirement. Few dogs can take possession of everything as I do. As I said, I sit between Him and Her so that They are delighted, but I only remain there if the weather is cold, or until the heater (installed for my comfort) has warmed up the interior to my liking. I nestle my head first against Him and then against Her, which pleases Them greatly; for They think how fond I am of Them. Just so; certainly I am; but also, their kness make an impromptu but nevertheless comfortable head-rest for me.

For a time only; there is no unalloyed bliss. My trouble is that I suffer from the possession of a periodic hot lie-me-down portion; so that presently, however rapt my enjoyment, the cushion underneath me gets too hot, and, largely owing to my thick coat, I begin to get hotter and hotter. Eventually I have to move. Where to? Obviously, onto the back seat, which being designed for no other purpose provides an area sufficient for my requirements, but only just.

On the back seat, which is softly cushioned with cool leather, I can spread myself lavishly. In vain do my Two wonder why beloved Too-Bade has deserted Them. What can such as They know, poor Humans, about the necessity for constant change and coolness which lie-me-down portions such as mine demand? By now, please note, I am spread all *de luxe*, lying on my back with all four utterly relaxed legs responding with abandon to every motion of the car, myself lost in bliss. Was ever a dog more happily rewarded? For now both of Them are shut in with me so that They cannot get away.

Alas, alas, bliss seldom lasts. Perfection, be it stated, does not properly accomodate itself to my requirements, even when on its best behaviour. Let me explain; only the other day, when I was happily located between Him and Her in the front seat, completely at ease, it happened! Presently as usual, my hot-seat began to get hotter and hotter. Yawning I arose, and prepared to leap gracefully over to the back seat. What did I see? Why, no less then three other Humans seated on *my* back seat, each looking more objectionable than I had thought possible even for Humans. I eyed them, one after the other, first mildly, then with impatience, then balefully, and at last with an annihilating glare. I gave an impatient whine. 'Shut up, you blighter!' He then said, unaware of my agonised feelings (for was I not getting everlastingly hotter?). Summoning all my forces I gave them yet another silent glare. What happened? One of them leant forward *and chucked me under the chin*!

Insulted, outraged, forgotten, betrayed, heartbroken, I crept away—no, not at all in high dudgeon—in a state of the lowest possible dudgeon to an insignificant, to an unworthy, to a shameful place, but blessedly cool: I sneaked, tail down, down to where His knobbly feet trample about when He is driving the car with clutches and brake-pedals and suchlike (including treading on me), to where a cool draught came in, and there I laid myself down, a shamed, a lonely but still indignant little dog, because certainly all three of those people should have been turned out to walk home to make room for me, instantly.

Can even worse things happen? Yes: for sometimes I am left behind altogether when They go motoring—do you get that? Yes, left alone, behind; and this although They know—none better—that there is nothing I like better than motoring. I have told Them so many, many times. I watch their every movement. I can read their thoughts before They actually decide to go out, so that long before the garage is unlocked I am *there* waiting, longing. Once I'm safely inside that car I of course feel that I am *there*, believing that no Human could ever be hard-hearted enough to turn me out again. Often I wait for an hour, two hours; They shall not go without me, I vow.

Yet sometimes—oh, desolation of desolation!—They gently lift me out of the car; They pet me, but firmly take me back to my basket (which I hate). They give me something nice to eat (which I never eat), and then They drive off leaving me listening—listening—feeling lonely, lonely.

Mostly, however, I claim my rights, and They obey. Generally speaking I approve of shopping, always providing that I can share in it. But when They leave me in the car I climb up on top of the back of the front seat and lamenting watch Them walk away. Have They forgotten that two waitresses (where They drink their coffee) dote on me, and better, pay tribute in snacks? When only She get out, I also disapprove, liking both with me always. I then express myself in a series of snuffly whines in ancient Chinese, and am told to 'shut up.'

But today the sun shines, and everything is perfect. My stage of hot-seatedness has now made me seek sanctuary on the back seat, which at present is cooling me down nicely. They on the front seat are wondering why I left Them. They have packed a picnic lunch, under my supervision, all very nice. They are going a long way. Better still. The road is smooth, the motion pleasant. Obviously I can now take my ease as I lie on my back, spread-eagled in blissful abandon, in a supreme and splendid relaxation. Each one of my four legs gently waggles and waves with the motion of the car. I have never a care in the world; and yet I graciously spare a thought for you, poor dear other Humans, who are feeling all taut and tight and tangled up with yourselves. Relax, relax into an abandoned relaxation like me. Picture me lying in this fashion with my car's back seat all to myself, caring nothing for other cars approaching from any angle, nothing for storm, snow, ice, fog (so long as the heater is working), nothing for the scenery or other people's conversation, caring nothing about anything! It is my personal wish that all my friends and admirers may soon find thenselves supremely relaxed in exactly the same way, each being driven in their own car with an entire back seat all to themselves. This is indeed Motoring into Superbia in superb style!

(Signed:) **TOO-BADE THE PEKE.**

LONDON IN WARTIME

The early years of the White Eagle Lodge—and of ANGELUS—*were also the years of the approach and outbreak of the Second World War. The work with which White Eagle and the Brothers in spirit charged their earthly brethren in these years, the 'years of fire' was set out in Ivan Cooke's now out-of-print book* THE WHITE BROTHERHOOD, *and has been described in a more general way in* THE STORY OF THE WHITE EAGLE LODGE. *Neither was the Lodge exempt from the common experience of war: in September 1940 the London 'home' of the Lodge was bombed and lay in ruins. Many readers will be familiar with White Eagle's words of imperturbable love spoken after this event.*

The pieces in this section do not refer directly to the spiritual work of the projection of the star in which White Eagle charged those on earth to cooperate; but they do, we hope, reflect some of the human experience of that time—the courage and humour demanded every day, to meet events that are now outside the experience of a whole generation.

Apart from the extract from the story 'Evolution', the following pieces are brief, occasional ones, written as editorials to ANGELUS. *'September Stirrings' dates from 1938 and has in fact no connection with the war at all—it is really meant as a foil for the pieces which follow. It is just a rather charming example of a request for material help in building up the work of the Lodge in London, one with which we hope readers will sympathise! The second piece is the editorial to the Christmas* ANGELUS, *written two months after the bombing of the London premises.*

SEPTEMBER STIRRINGS.—These are the stale days of July, when Kensington begins to look very much as though a couple of days at the sea—or even beneath—might freshen things; yet these same pages will go out to our readers when September comes round, a vast space of days away. Perish the thought though, that this particular number of Angelus should lack vigour. The Kensington air, the house agents say, comes laden with health and spiced with ozone of the North Sea. South Winds blow to us the scent of Surrey flowers and heathlands. There certainly never was such air! ... Good! We now take a deep breath.... With the following result:—

The Organ. Observant members of our congregation have doubtless noticed that our regular organ was replaced for a month by a younger scion of the race—an organic pup, as it were—known to the music lover as a harmonium. No, our organ was not on holiday. Sundry defects obtruded themselves in its internal organs; an organ expert was called in; he said the case was desperate, but we said we didn't mind about the case—it was the inside that delivered the music. We called in another expert, who said the trouble was undoubtedly organic. We agreed. He said that if allowed to continue the organ would become completely disorganised, and that there was nothing for it but its removal to an organ hospital. Surgical attention, and four weeks recuperation would work wonders.

And now our organ has come back to us; and trailing, like Mary, not a little lamb, but a by no means little bill, which makes us somewhat thoughtful. Would anyone like to help us with that bill? Or shall we organise an appeal!

We take another deep breath. . . . But no; on second thoughts perhaps the air was almost *too* bracing . . . but on the summer air there comes to us the scent of flowers—and the thought of candles, incense, and oil for the altar lamps. The beauty and fitness of the Lodge is dear to all who worship and serve therein. This we know; and for many months this has been maintained by the help of two of our members, who have not only contributed largely towards the cost of flowers (for there are seven altars) but also for candles, incense, and sanctuary oil. We feel that there are many others who would wish to share in this cost, had they the opportunity, and thus lighten the burden. Contributions will be for these purposes alone, and will be gratefully received.

DECEMBER 1940.—This is the fifth Christmas Number of ANGELUS. Three times has the Christmas Number of ANGELUS appeared in duplicated form, and last Christmas, to inaugurate the printing of our journal, we produced (with some pride) our first printed number of ANGELUS. The venture has justified itself more than ever in these war-time days when the speading of the teaching overrides purely material considerations . . . although ANGELUS has yet to pay its way; and we go forward with high hopes despite the times . . . Or, shall we say, because of the times and the Christmas Message that they bring.

We are well aware of adverse factors. The secretarial and office work of the Lodge (which includes the preparation of this journal) is done partly in Kent, partly in Hampshire and in part in Edinburgh, a factor making neither for efficiency nor convenience. It is a grief also that we cannot have our Annual Christmas Tree in Pembroke Hall, a joyful episode to which we have usually looked forward at this Season. Gifts of money, however, will be gladly received, and be distributed as Christmas gifts to those in need, as in previous years . . . and next year, we will make up for all these things . . . *Next Year.* . . . !

Which brings us nearer to our point. . . . We would stress that quality of hopefulness in the human heart, a hopefulness due not at all to wishful thinking, but rather an intuitive faculty which will not be denied. Indeed, the more developed the soul, the more richly and strongly does hopefulness well from the deeps of the heart; the more does this hopefulness reveal of godliness in all life.

We clear the ground as we press forward. The more developed the man, the stronger he grows in hope, faith and joy. Because of these things, God must be hopeful, as full of faith in humanity as man is in God, and, therefore, God is joyful because he is ever bringing forth good. Good out of evil—that is always the eventual outworking of calamities, sorrows, cruelty, darkness: a fact that history, in its broader aspects, will as certainly corroborate, as history will, when time brings to it dispassion, assert that this present war should never have been—so we believe.

Should never have been; the war should have been averted. But because the war is here upon us, let us take heart. Humanity has either chosen or been thrust out upon a steep hard path. That progress which might have been accomplished gradually and gently is now being purchased by fears and blood and tears. Is the price asked too high for what the future promises? Surely, surely not! Surely all is going to prove a thousand times worth while when man and God together are labouring to bring forth good

out of present evils.

We are rising from ashes of our past to forge our future. What if we fail, and selfishness still prevails? That rests with each one of us—with you and me . . . and God. We must not, shall not fail. With quiet certitude we shall go forward.

In this spirit of assurance we would wish our readers, old and new, all the good wishes of the Season. The building which housed the White Eagle Lodge has been reduced to splintered rubble and laid waste. The Lodge goes on, is already finding a new home, more convenient, worthy and beautiful than the last. So also with this shattering civilisation of ours which already reveals many a fault, shortcoming and injustice of which we were previously ignorant or blind. The old 'bottles,' be they social, economic, political or religious—cannot contain the wine of the New Age. We shall create the better world wherein war and poverty and injustice are no more; and you and I are called to labour.

With thankfulness then, we wish you, one and all, true happiness at this Christmas Season of high hope. Soon will the night break and the dawn glow.

May God bless you all!

The background to the next piece is the blackout of wartime London.

[*February 1943*] WHAT WILL *YOU* DO when the bells ring out the tidings of an Armistice? Oh, you don't know—go mad, dance, sing, shout—drink a toast to something or somebody, open your last tin of something or other, gobble up your butter ration—you simply don't know, of course. Nobody does. Perhaps a large number of people will feel very quiet, awed, and maybe sorrowful when they think of the cost of the past years. Many will find relief in tears, both of thankfulness and grief; and rightly, too. Many will simply pray with prayer too deep for words.

But one reaction will be universal—the desire to show forth light. Windows will blaze forth, streets will be lit, cars will loose their direful headlights. We shall glow with delight as we see light shine forth again. This will be a deep and true instinct and longing thus seeking expression. We have plumbed the depths of emotional agony, mental and spiritual desolation. With profound gratitude we turn again to that Light which is a primal necessity for our whole being. . . .

Therefore our blazing windows and streets will symbolise a personal and national desire for liberty, freedom, peace—or, in other words, for a greater personal, social and national enlightenment, or coming of the Light; and we shall best express our thankfulness, when we have taken thought on the matter—and the first emotions quieten down—in seeking some means by which we can more fully and more worthily serve the Forces of the Light.

[*June 1943*] THE CHORISTRY. Outside the editorial den at the Lodge (we cannot honestly call it a sanctum) is a kind of balcony or sun trap, where dead leaves congregate in the winter and dust in the summer. Over and above this there grows a tree, an ash tree! A tree that is forthright, well nourished and not in the least despondent about its situation in an abandoned garden, or about the war in general; and this although it cannot help but listen-in several times daily, when so many loudspeakers blare away in the vicinity. Its immediate outlook is somewhat gloomy, however. Scarred and deserted dwellings backed by overgrown gardens are not the happiest things to gaze down upon; and again, ominous gaps lurk between those houses—gaps which were once sprawling masses of rubble, furnishings, clothing, anything—gaps which once spelt tragedy on some dark wintry night.

Our tree saw these things happen, but puts a lusty face on it. It must have many friends. Some of its leaves come peeping down to participate in the Sunday Services in the chapel at the Lodge—green and graceful leaves making wavings and beckonings, seen dimly through the grime upon our windows in these cleaner-shortage days. We glance up to see something greenly-gracious reminding us of bright meadow and woodlands, and of other ash trees in their natural hedgerow or copse. A lovely tree, the ash. What a strong heart must this one have to root and grow in Kensington!

But then, its friends! We had forgotten those friends, numerous enough to put heart into any tree. They come, winged choristers as they are, to tell their ash-tree about wondrous things—of springtime in the streets and gardens, of green grass in London parks. He listens, leaves rustling, to their glad news. Such news, such songs and such songsters keep him sound and strong of heart. There are no dolours, no depression among those songsters... and yet, they own nothing—cannot even afford a penny upon a newspaper to make themselves miserable with. They do not listen-in; so far as they are concerned the world is healthful and wholesome. Even cats are off their mind. In consequence their song reflects only joyousnes and peace, to which we poor war-raddled folk listen with a catch at the breath and the heart at the sheer lightheartedness of it all.

Yes, many at the Lodge listen. For the songs come stealing across our Sunday services. The singers sing with us, they praise and worship, naturally, so sweetly—as might we, were we simpler folk, more akin to our tree and bird. Hearken—just above a thrush is singing—singing—singing—*now*! Its notes ride high above the chatter of the editorial typewriter. What a song to broadcast—and what a message to broadcast to the world!

Many of the 'Little Tales' that Ivan Cooke wrote during the war reflect wartime experiences, and several touch on the transition to the greater reality, the world of light, of souls violently flung out of the physical life. The story from which the following extract is taken, however, does not deal directly with these experiences—but we felt that the close of the little fable, written in 1943, reflected some of the same tenderness.

EVOLUTION.—Then the Angel, greatly compassionate, bent down; and the man, trusting, laid his hand within that of the Angel. And together they set forth—together. Whither? Ah, the strangest path they followed, and yet a path that all men must some day walk, but only when an angel comes to companion them. For they travelled from the outer life into the inner—from the outer world into that strange secret world that lies within each man, and which none find until the moment cometh. Within, within the man's own self they went.

The strangest journey. For within the head of that man burned a feverish thing called brain or mind, shot through and ravelled by a thousand torturous thoughts, hungers, longings, questings, and desires that dominated him, claiming to be wisdom, knowledge, power, omniscience. They passed it by. With averted head the man passed it by, for therein lay that which he did not at that moment care to look upon.

They went deeper, to where strange sub-conscious thought-forces were stored, forces which governed and ruled the workings of the body, and shaped it, giving it its aspects and habits, moulding it to strength or weakness, sickness or health, as a potter moulds the clay. And therein man saw how he had shaped himself, and whence came the current of his thoughts, and those desires which had made him what he was. He saw also a little cave called 'Memory,' wherein was stored a few jewels and much rubbish, but therein he did not at that time care to look overmuch.

They went deeper, seeming to enter some mighty powerhouse. Man saw how the airs that sweep the seas, the valleys and the hills, entered into him to nourish and sustain his life; he saw the glow of life thay brought to him with each deep inhalation; and the marvel of the circulation and replenishment of the blood. They went deeper, and he heard the pulse of his unresting heart. Great wonders were revealed to him, greater than he had ever known, concerning his own being, its governance and sustenance.

And then they entered a secret place, like to a little cave, where all was still and very silent, where no noise of earthliness penetrated—where in the centre lay (as a shrine is set up in a sanctuary)... a Rose. A Rose most fair to see, glowing with life, with colour and with fragrance, and radiating forth light; and dewed with purity was that Rose, for naught had stained it.

Then man saw the Angel draw near, and all His winged being seemed to bow down, as if before something too holy for aught but worship; and looking closer the man saw, cradled in the heart of the Rose, a tiny babe most fair to see—the fairest sight in earth or heaven, he thought; and thought also that he would bend to kiss the babe, and then found himself afraid. And heard the Angel say softly, 'Never in the mind—always in the heart.... The Rose blooms unseen in the heart of Man. The heart is ever the shrine, the Rose the cradle. Hail, little Babe-Christ, Saviour and Redeemer, born this holy day!'

TWO LONGER STORIES

As well as the short fables that we have seen so far, the 'Little Tales of the Spirit' included some rather longer stories, one or two of which (the ones not too unorthodox in outlook!) were accepted for radio broadcast by the BBC under the pen-name, John Ein. The two stories here are both from ANGELUS.

The Mirrored Land

THE MIRROR in its golden frame had hung above John Graham's fireplace for fifty years. John Graham had first seen it when he and Constance had been on their honeymoon in Italy, during a month of golden days of sunshine and happiness. Since then the years had slipped away, while the mirror had silently waited upon them both—watched and shared their lives, becoming looked upon as a sympathetic friend and a confidant of both. Long ago as it was, John remembered how they both had fallen for that mirror at the first glance, framed as it was so subtly, so suitably, so graciously, and itself offering so gracious a reflection to all who looked therein. For some mirrors are harsh and brittle, and cruel with those they encounter, as soulless as some brazen minx of a woman, over-emphasising the furrows of time, deepening, exaggerating the crowsfeet around the eyes, and every imprint of weariness and care; while others are kindly, softening and brightening those whom they reflect, respecting that inner assurance we all retain with advancing years that we look somehow as young as we feel, and that graying hair and lines upon the face, so long as they are kindly lines, can lend it grace. Such a mirror was this *par excellence*; and never was such a mirror for reflecting flowers. Whenever a vase of flowers was placed upon the mantelpiece beneath it, the mirror took them to itself and gave them back again into the room—their freshness, form, colour, substance—so that their charm was enhanced. This was the reason that John had placed a jar of Christmas roses before it as an offering before a shrine that very day. For year by year had not Constance offered a similar gift of roses to their mirror, or rather *her* mirror, for it had been she who had first discovered its rare qualities—even as their mirror in return had reflected *her* quality back again into their room, back into their wedded lives.

'What a woman Constance was,' John thought, 'for getting the feel of things!' When they made some purchase, always she wanted something that someone had wrought with loving care, some product of skilled and scrupulous craftsmanship. 'Because,' she said (and he had laughed at her at the time, but later learnt how true she was) 'there's a something about things like that which comes out into the room, and which I can feel.'

To think that he had ever teased her for that fancy, and would have chosen rather some factory mass-produced suite or a picture reeled off by the printing press in its thousands! Why, the very chair he was sitting in now—some craftsman four centuries ago had conceived and wrought it in English oak as lustrous in its homely way as the sunlight which had called the original tree into being. With delight he studied a watercolour over the bureau (itself a treasure Constance had discovered) with its sheen of bluebells spread over a woodland dell, thinking that in itself the picture sounded the call of spring—yes, even on this bleak winter evening when outside the ground lay rimed with frost, and a bitter east wind snarled around the house.

He glanced at the carpet on which his slippered feet rested, noted the intricacies of its design. Some Eastern craftsman labouring for the means to keep life in a body mostly skin and bone, had conceived and fashioned the carpet, and had patterned it with some marvel of artistry—had wrought *himself* into it body and soul; so that, long dead and dust, he lived again and was beheld in this his craftsmanship. His was only temporary immortality, of course; for some day when John was dead (often of late he had thought of his own death without actually facing up to it) the carpet would pass to others who might not appreciate its worth as John did. But then he had been taught the loving art of appreciation by Constance—his wife Constance.

Yes, still his, though dead these many years, still his very own. For she lived in him; she still lived with him; her presence and character had so infused themselves into every article in this her room that to John all, all, was a reflection of her. But then they were only inanimate things, while he was a living man, and in his life and memories she had a deeper and more intimate life. Not at first, though; time had been when a storming sorrow and sense of unutterable loss had barred her away from him, and penned him in a cell of unutterable loneliness. That was a bad time, sad and bad, and ... unnecessary.

Yes, it need never have been. For when he had dared to probe his loneliness to its source, he had found that source rooted in the resentment he bore—to someone, Something ... that had taken her away ... to God perhaps? Yes, then he had been so sick in mind and sore in heart that the creature had dared to challenge its Creator to beat himself against the inevitable. Not now, though; why, perhaps all that had happened had been good, inasmuch as it had taught and mellowed him; certainly as the years had passed it had brought a sense of her presence, closer sometimes than if she had actually sat in her chair facing his across the hearth. For then his thoughts often wandered far away, whereas now they centred upon her in a blessed communion.

He rose to tend the fire, scrupulously sweeping every particle of dust beneath the grate. Once Constance could never make him do that to her liking. Often he hadn't troubled. But now he never neglected this task, because to do so would be seeming to fail her. For a while John Graham remained standing, gazing into the mirror that was so charged with memories.

Never before had it seemed so lustrous, so purely luminous . . . never before! The reflection of the Christmas roses came back into the room as if they possessed some inward light; the mirrored room seemed as if newly illumined so that as never before the spirit of the craftsmen who had made it homely and beautiful shone forth; and the reflected face of John seemed happier and more peaceful than ever before, so that the years fell from it. Or rather, as if through the mask of those years the face of the young husband who had spent that joyous month in Italy looked back into his. A queer trick of fancy, John thought.

Constance then had been only a little bit of a thing. He had often teased her about her stature. Ah, but she would look more tiny still in the dress women wore today. For in that long ago women went about huddled up with clothes, laced in at the waist and bulged out elsewhere in the queerest way. Not that extravagance of dress had been able to hide Constance's daintiness or make her other than sweet and alluring from her golden crown of hair to her dainty feet. How he had worshipped at her shrine in those

youthful days. But never had she seemed so dear as now—now that he was old and alone . . . so much had he learnt since then.

Strangely youthful, strangely vigorous looked that reflection of his in the mirror on that Christmas night. More like himself in his prime than that white-haired man which had faced him each morning in his shaving mirror for more years than he could remember. Some trick of fancy, of course, or of those eyes of his—which had been growing troublesome of late. He was looking now at the reflection of the curtained windows, behind which lay that frost-bitten garden, remembering that outside ran a crazy path, in summer-time bordered with delphiniums, the blue of them matching but not excelling the blue of her eyes. That bed of flowers had been her special and tender care, so much so that afterwards . . . afterwards he could not bear to look upon those delphiniums and had rooted them out. This had happened during his bad time. Afterwards he had replanted the delphiniums and loved them the more with each passing year. Why, between two old fruit trees at the end a hammock was slung, where she would read or drowse during summer hours . . . that is, until she heard his step, when she would fling herself out and come running to clasp her arms about his neck, to press her lips to his. Always when he returned would she break into that little run of hers—always that welcome shone in her eyes and upon her face.

These were sweet memories to cherish, to live with in this sere and weary age which had come upon him. These alone brought her close.

Again his eyes met those of his mirrored reflection. The steady, clear gray eyes of his young manhood gazed into his; and, most strangely, that mirrored form now wore a gray jacket suit of rough tweed which he had worn—when?—surely upon that same honeymoon—the very jacket he had worn when first they saw the mirror in that street in old Florence, and he and Constance had bargained for its purchase. A 'Norfolk' suit they had called it then—though why Norfolk he didn't know.

Now the mirror had grown lustrous and luminous beyond belief, so that the room it reflected shone with a brightness which turned the room in which he stood into a shadowed thing; and that image of himself still faced him, and seemed to inveigle him, to tempt him to reach out, to touch it; it seemed to offer itself as if it could convey to him something of his youthful manhood once contact could be made. Hesitating, tentatively, he reached out, and a hand that felt strong and vigorous met his—touched, yes, and clasped his firmly, warmly, compellingly—and drew him onwards, inwards into the mirror itself.

And behold, that mirror was no longer there; no surface of glass impeded his passage; he seemed to reach in and through the mirror, to step into that luminous room beyond—into that room that was so like his own . . . and more, into that figure so like and yet so unlike himself that hand drew him. The two merged, they came together, the old man and the new, and then the young John Graham was no longer standing within that mirror-room, but only old John Graham, by now feeling strangely renewed, strangely and insistently young again. For John had absorbed his mirrored image unto himself.

It was not the queerness of all this which dominated his thoughts at this moment, but a sense of expectancy which overrode all else. He felt that something tremendous was about to happen! His mind was as clear cut and keen as ever it had been. This could be no old man's dream. Rather he felt as if he had awakened from some long drawn-out dream, to feel never more awake, never more keyed up, never more observant in his life. He was aware of the minutest detail within that mirror-room, aware that everything in it had come to life as never before. Once they had sensed that all those furnishings they had chosen were infused by something of the dead craftsmen who had created them. Now they all testified to their creative art and skill. The bluebells in the woodland were actually blooming, the woodland itself fragrant with flowers and the smell of the good wet earth, the scene warm and quick with sunlight. The carpet was become a living harmony of soft graduated colour, texture, pattern and beauty. More than all this, there was no shadowed corner, no dullness or drabness in that mirror-room. Even the curtains before the windows glowed as if lit by some radiance outside and beyond them—and then, as John looked again, he was sure that they were warmed by sunlight, that sunlight was shining upon that garden outside. Common sense whispered that this was an impossibility, that it was a wintry night. Yet such was his sense of expectancy that nothing seemed impossible, that anything might happen.

He strode towards the windows and the curtains were warm to his touch as he flung them aside with a hand suddenly grown brown, strong, youthful, and looked out upon a sunkissed garden—upon level green sward, upon June sunlight falling upon a path edged with blue, blue delphiniums. All, all as he had expected in this supreme hour! for this nothing could prove too wonderful! He flung the french windows wide, and the garden came to greet him in great waves of warmth and light, colour and aroma—all the essence, the spiritual quality of that garden. He stepped out into it. Never had such a sense of exhaltation as this quickened his being.

Yet there was more to come. Every fibre of him told him that. Down that path waited his supreme moment. Quietly and steadily he went forward to meet it, down the path to where the hammock was once slung in the long ago summer, down the path up which Constance used to come running to meet him . . . long, long ago.

And then he heard her call, heard her quick feet upon the stones. He stopped, waiting, his heart pounding, his eyes misted, yet never missing a scrap of her. For she came; seeming to him as youthful and beautiful as spring itself, her hair golden as the sunlight (and once it had grown thin, dulled and gray, and her dear face lined by suffering), her eyes blue and shining, her hands outstretched, her lips uplifted to meet his—his wife, his all! light of his heart and of his life that she had always been . . . she came!

The Wedding Ring

NEVER SINCE the day when Herbert (even then plump, and round and comfortable) had married her in the old parish church, had that wedding ring left Mrs. Jones' third finger—never! and now, as she often said, 'Please God, it never would!' And indeed it didn't seem likely, although she had feared once that, owing to the increasing girth of her finger, it might have to be cut off. But this phase passed—or shall we say, dispersed? Which was fortunate indeed, because Mrs. Jones had settled once and for all that the ring must never, never come off. Year by year the idea had strengthened that her wedded happiness with Herbert was so indissolubly bound up and intertwined with the ring—so to speak—that to lose contact with that dull and worn circlet of gold was to lose happiness itself.

For Herbert had always been 'that kind' with her; even though he had become gray and frail and worn, she was still 'his gal'; he was always tender and thoughtful with her—in spite of the fact that men are naturally trying creatures and there is no altering them, and they will get nasty if they are nagged. Herbert had a quiet plodding way of getting through life which somehow suited her own gentle nature. He grew his 'taters' with immeasurable care, tended his 'bits of flowers' with a yearning devotion almost motherly, lavished upon his garden and upon her that tenderness which might have expended itself upon a child, if only . . . .

'But, you see,' as Mrs. Jones would say in one of those intimate woman-to-woman confidences over a cup of tea, 'There hadn't never been no children.' Once—ah, *once* there had come a promise and expectation which filled them both with delight and excitement.... And then (and Mrs. Jones' faded eyes would mist over) there had been that accident. 'Nothing in itself, but'—then the conversation grew intimate indeed.

Since then things had taken a turn for the better. Herbert had 'got on' a bit—not according to his deserts, of course, but still 'a bit'—so that he was able to retire and devote that attention to his 'taters' to which business had hitherto been an unwanted distraction. Then he and 'the Missus' settled down to be real comfortable; and then it was that Missus wanted a bit of help in the house, and that was how Gladys first came to them.

Gladys, you see, was brought up in a Home—an Orphanage, to be exact. You could guess it at a glance, because she had that sort of 'square' look—like an unnecessarily ugly pair of boots—which Orphanage children always had. 'Nobody wasn't to know about this,' said Mrs. Jones, 'none of the neighbours or folk like that, because they might point a finger at her.' It was understood that Gladys came from 'the country,' an origin vague enough to satisfy anybody. Anyway, nobody took much interest in Gladys, as they watched her spare and scraggy figure go by on her 'afternoon orf.' 'Mrs. Jones won't make nothing of the likes of her,' they said, and sniffed. They also had tried to train 'them girls,' ungrateful hussies that they were! 'Better by half have a good honest char.'

Not that Gladys minded what they thought. The likes of them! After that orphanage her new menage seemed princely, and every kindness shown by Mrs. Jones—and they were many—shone with re-doubled radiance, while the cottage magnified itself into a palace, and (as romance budded) she herself into a fairy princess gracing a home *exactly like that* which would one day be hers. Not that Gladys knew much about fairy princesses; they never visited orphanages, it seems. But she had had her dreams. And in Gladys' dream there walked many a time a Fairy Prince.

So princely a prince! So true, so good! and not unlike Missus's Mr. Jones, you know, in disposition, as kind, as gentle, as thoughtful. *He* (her prince) wouldn't never clump a gal, nor yet set about her, verbally or otherwise. *He* wouldn't age like Mr. Jones, or get bent or gray, but always be in the prime of youth and manhood. Sometimes even he wore a Lifeguardsman's uniform, and was then at his most splendid! Sometimes he was only a bobby, smart and solid (as bobbies are), and he and she would meet—by accident like! And then a whole train of wonderful events would follow, all somehow tending to wedded happiness in a couple of rooms somewhere in fairyland, where she would fry fish suppers for her prince!

Sometimes during 'afternoons orf' she would glance this way or that with a curious feeling that her prince was very nearly come into her life. Just around that corner he would be waiting. . . ? No—not that corner. Then surely around the next? No, and again no. Then on the next afternoon off she would surely meet him—or on the next?

By this time Gladys was rounding, growing plumper, filling out. Rude boys (the very antithesis of the prince) ceased to call ribaldly as she passed, and instead became goggley and sheepish. They, too, were growing up, it seems; not that she took notice of the likes of them. She was pledged, she felt, and wouldn't have no truck with nobody until her 'Mr. Right' claimed her. And Mr. Right wasn't so long in coming after all.

For the bugles blew, and then the brass bands blared forth so brazenly that they stole the senses away and sent Britain's youth with lilting heart to join up—thousands upon thousands they marched to war; and each had a mother, dear God, each had a clean manhood which might have blossomed out into wife and child and home and happiness! Soon they filled the little town where Gladys lived with a khaki throng. Now was the splendour of romance come. No longer need a girl demean herself by walking out with one of 'them fellers'—not that Gladys had ever intended to, mind you. A girl could pick and choose these days—not that Gladys would demean herself to pick and choose ('demean' came from the vocabulary of Mrs. Jones, by the way).

But if somebody out of these soldiers should prove to be *the* prince. . . . Ah, then what might not happen? For he would be so honourable (another gem from Mrs. Jones) that she could surely trust him.

(You think you can guess the end of the story by now, do you? You've heard stories just like this before, and they usually end in much the same way? Yes, I know. But there's a twist here, a kindly gentle human thing at the end. So please wait).

After all it was the prince who walked right into Gladys one foggy night; literally, they bumped into each other. He proved to be a khaki-clad corporal, full fed, fresh, and inclined to be beefy—all of which attributes seemed princely indeed to the bedraggled Gladys. They walked out, not once but several times, she in a delirium of happiness. Mrs. Jones scented romance, became tepidly anxious, but not unduly so. 'British soldiers don't do that sort of thing, Herbert,' she said crisply and clearly, and he chirped back, 'Well, I only said that there's slugs on every cabbage patch, me dear, and you want to watch out for 'em.'

But in her heart Mrs. Jones knew that British soldiers sometimes *did* do that sort of unnameable thing. But what could she do about it now that Gladys was nineteen? Nothing, you see. Girls are only young once.

Nothing! There was nothing to be done when at last the bugles blew and the brass band blared the prince's regiment to the station to entrain for France. Gladys watched them march by from an upper window through streaming tears. With all her heart she grudged the loss of her prince. Other men, perhaps, might go to war, but not *he*. Then the weeks flew by, and the prince wrote only occasionally— 'as real heroes can only be expected to write,' Gladys thought; and then, like a dream the giant maw of war swallowed him up . . . for ever. Perhaps his name appears upon a roll of honour somewhere, on some village war memorial—for all this happened twenty-odd years ago. Perhaps some mother carried a scar in her heart to her dying day. Nobody knows. Like a figure in a dream he appears out of the unknown, lives, loves and then departs.

But not wholly, not altogether. Because as more months passed, a suspicion which became a dreadful certainty stole upon Gladys. She knew then what had happened to her; and it was the worst possible. What would everyone think? Worst of all, what would Missus Jones think? She hardened herself. Her heart was broke, she thought, and this came but as another blow. Gawd, but she didn't care! She wasn't going to let on to nobody, she wasn't. She'd keep her mouth shut to her dying day, and she hoped it wasn't far off . . . so there!

And she didn't let on—not she. She didn't care for nobody no more. She was going to keep on at the Jones, because they were that innocent they wouldn't notice nothing, she thought. Besides, when you see a person every day, what might be obvious to some becomes not so noticeable, and she took very good care about the sharp eyes of 'nosey parkers' outside the house. Again the weeks passed, and the months. Nobody guessed, nobody knew, she believed—perhaps nobody did, until one night Mrs. Jones woke up and heard someone groaning—groaning, with an occasional whimper of pain. 'Do you hear that,' she whispered, and Herbert answered (as he usually did answer), 'I'm listening, my dear.'

Mrs. Jones bundled out of bed and rushed into Gladys' room, spurred by a dreadful suspicion. The door banged in Herbert's face. Then it opened. Sharp staccato orders issued forth. Herbert must go for the doctor—at once! Hot water in vast quantities was required—at once! Herbert must place himself wholly under her orders—at once!

Then ensued a period of dumb and helpless waiting for Herbert. Without a bit of baccy, he doesn't know how he would have got on during that night.

Somehow he felt he oughtn't to be there—oughtn't, in fact, to be anywhere at all. Meanwhile, what transpired behind that door?

Not what you might think. There was stern stuff within young Gladys that forbade tears and confession. 'She wouldn't demean herself; she wasn't going to tell nothing to nobody, she wasn't: wasn't nobody's business but hers.' Shame too overwhelming for speech silenced her, chilled her tenderness for even the Missus. 'She didn't want no doctor, she didn't. Let them only leave her alone—that's all she wanted.'

Not until Mrs. Jones told her that the doctor had been sent for and was on his way did she wilt. Then her hardihood broke down. She pleaded, she besought. Again and again, 'She didn't want no doctor—she didn't want nobody to know.' If only 'he' had known, *this* wouldn't have happened. He would have given her a proper ring, all right, and then she wouldn't have cared. But he was dead . . . *dead!*' Oh, doleful, wailing cry! 'And now the doctor would go and tell everybody about her—all them old gals!—and they'd. . . . Lord knew what they wouldn't say!' And again, wailingly, '*He'd* have given her a ring, he would, all straight and proper.'

(I like to recall what followed, not only because of the act in itself, which was good and human, but because of its outcome. By reason of this act something of absorbing interest and appeal crept into the love and lives of Herbert and his wife—a helpless child . . . Gladys' child! Because Gladys and her child stayed with them afterwards. They lived long, and Gladys cared for them both in their old age—there was good stuff in Gladys, it wanted bringing out, and kindness did it. Maybe that which I have to tell doesn't sound so great a thing as it actually was? Perhaps plenty of folk would have done the like, and without a thought. But here's the difference. Mrs. Jones thought first—oh, yes, long and deep and fearfully—of what might happen afterwards. One does not risk the shattering of a lifetime's happiness lightly).

And then? . . . And then she drew that wedding ring, worn so thin, so scratched and dulled by the years, from off her finger—so easily, so deftly, for work and years had worn the fingers thin and fragile—and slipped the ring on to the finger of Gladys—where *he* might have placed *his* ring, but hadn't. 'For you, my dear, for you!' said old Mrs. Jones, 'and with an old woman's blessing. For somehow I know that this is a blessed thing we two are doing.' And the old woman with so big a heart slipped an arm round Gladys and held her tight.

THOUGHTS ON THE WORK OF THE LODGE

The following are from STELLA POLARIS, *and give a vision of the significance of the work of the White Eagle Lodge. In the second piece, the 'special reason' behind the lighthouse symbol was that it was adopted as the motif of the Million Penny Fund, begun in order to raise funds to pay off the mortgage of the London Lodge. The third piece is an editorial of the same time, on a general theme.*

[*February 1955*] ANNIVERSARY.—Long ago (in February, 1936, to be exact) someone wrote to us after the opening and dedication of the White Eagle Lodge. The writer, who had been present, saw the Lodge in a vision as a lighthouse shedding its beam upon all wayfarers. Year before then, before anyone had thought of founding a Lodge, a man had stood before an open window in another part of London, and pointed in the direction of where the Lodge would some day be, saying that he saw there a great light in the sky, which took the form of a six-pointed star. This man was a wise seer. That star, he said, was the herald of a Temple of the Star which would come into being and some day radiate light, truth and healing to mankind. Years later the Lodge was established at Pembroke Hall, its first home. She who had listened to the Wise Man subsequently became a member of the Lodge. Its symbol, as is known, is the six-pointed star, and as was predicted its work has been to radiate light, truth and healing.

How has this radiation been sent forth? By means of its every activity, is the obvious answer. The Sunday Services, the Talks to students, the Brotherhood, the Contact and Absent Healing, Stella Polaris and the books—all these are surely methods of sending out the light. Yes—or rather, they have provided means to a more important *end*. They contact only a limited number of people; yet the influence for which the Lodge is a channel spreads to all, and has no bounds or limitation. Why is this?

Because the Lodge was originally formed to function as a *receiving station* for the light. It is also a *transforming* station, in that it brings down the angelic and spiritual radiations (they too are distinct) to a more earthly wavelength. Having received and transformed this light it is also a *radiating* station, because every one of its activities is utilised for radiating or broadcasting this angelic and spiritual light to mankind. Therefore its radiation of light is not confined to the comparatively few worshippers at the Lodge, or to the thousands of people who read its books. Its ideal, its purpose and its work are world-wide, affecting all people of good will; it is in very truth shedding its beams on every human wayfarer and by so doing is working for the salvation of the Soul of the World. This, briefly, is the reason for the White Eagle Lodge and its Daughter Lodges.

[*April 1955*] CONCERNING LIGHTHOUSES.—A lighthouse is presumably a building which must be built (or founded) on a rock before it can withstand the assaults of storm and sea. Its supreme function is to give light to storm-tossed mariners, and so warn them against rocks or shoals and guide them to safe harbourage. The first duty of the men of the lighthouse is the tending of its light, which must never grow dim or fail. That light is always situated at the top of the lighthouse, where it shines forth to all. Its attendants reach the light by means of a spiral or circular ladder or stairway, which in effect seems to climb from earth to heaven—or so it appears to the casual visitor or stranger lacking a calling to be faithful to the light.

A lighthouse, surprisingly enough, is made in the image of man: and we are bidden, so it is said, to found or establish our house upon a rock. Built on sand it will surely be destroyed. It is also our charge to tend that light faithfully—that light of man's spirit which can shine out to warn others of dangers ahead and point the way to safe harbourage. In short, we men are—or should be—lighthouses at the service of all storm-tossed mariners or wayfarers. Our paramount duty, therefore, is to tend the light—that light of ours which is the spiritual intelligence sited, we are told, at the crown of man's head.

To tend that light we must climb a spiral stairway tending ever upwards. Man's spiritual growth, we are told, is ever in the form of a spiral—a stairway, if you will, climbing upwards from incarnation to incarnation, from initiation to initiation. To tend and to cherish his Christ light is not only the first duty but the whole mission of man.

Why does all this about lighthouses appear at this juncture? Because it has a special reason and significance just now. Elsewhere in this issue of Stella Polaris you will find this significance set forth. But not here—here your editor has to hoard his space as a miser does his gold. Here he comes to his full stop.

Then for the interim let us say to ourselves, "Let your light so shine before men. . . .'

[*April 1946*] THE GRACE OF GOD.—An old fashioned phrase? Don't let us be too sure. For possibly there lies in the words the one reality to be found in this world of dream and shadow - the way to peace of heart. For inner peace, a peace which transcends our outer circumstances as daylight transcends the darkness, can be found only by means of this same grace of God.

How then does a soul seek this grace of God? Not by flogging the mind to a supreme and continuous effort to rule its own waywardness; not by any mental process, but rather by a letting go of mental strain, a surrender and a forgetting of the trouble, sorrow and pain to which we cling so tightly, and a resting of the soul upon God.

This is not to be conceived as some form of spiritual inertia; rather is it an acceptance of the Creator as the fundamental reality pervading all life, and a realisation that all else is unimportant in comparison, so that one's house of life is built upon the eternal rock, instead of upon temporal sands.

The grace of God is a permeating essence which pervades the inner being and externalises itself into the outer life. It comes first as a deep pool of quietness within, which outer worries and troubles have no power to disturb; and the influence of that quietness rises up into the mind and thoughts, habits and feelings of daily life, so that tact, kindliness and wisdom become a natural and effortless expression of that which lies within. For now the pivot of our being has changed. Whereas before self and self-interest was that pivot, now we are unconsciously aligned with an eternal purpose which encompasses a whole universe.

The supreme reality of this grace of God can only be understood by those who have found it - or whom it has found; for it is ever seeking expression through men. But perhaps something of its reality can be conveyed by the analogy of spring supplanting winter's harshness, of light and growth triumphing over darkness, decay and death. The coming of the grace of God is the breaking of the spring in the wintry soul of man, its budding and its flowering. Some day it will produce that spiritual sustenance upon which other spiritually starving souls can feed. And come it will, some day, to each and every soul; for the whole plan of creation, and the whole purpose of life with every man, is to prepare his soul against that coming; and all that man undergoes serves to break and till the soil of the soul in preparation for that great end.

EPILOGUE

We end this anthology with a return to the gentle sunshine with which we began.

Kiss of the Sun

THE SNOWDROPS say it happened during February. The golden crocuses, however, are certain that it happened during March. Certain it is that somewhere about that time the great Sun bent down to kiss the Earth, bidding her to awaken.

Whereupon the Earth answered that she just couldn't! She was still frozen; what she really wanted was a thicker covering of snow to keep her warm. And down she settled for another winter snooze. But not a bit of it! Everyone of her creatures already knew about this springtide kiss coming from the Sun; they had shared in it. And such a flittering took place among the ants and bees and such fluttering among the birds that you would have thought spring had arrived already, while every one of them, every creature cried out to Earth, 'Hurry! hurry! hurry! or we shall all starve when winter comes again. Hurry now to fill up our storehouses—all of us, everyone of us depend on you.'

Then came a warmer, sunnier kiss upon Earth's cheek from the Sun above, and another bidding to bestir herself. And so she did, being a good Earth.

But first she told the Sun about her troubles—about a race of men so ignorant, so plundering in ignorance that they robbed her of her minerals and her fertility, and sullied and polluted all her form and frame. What could Earth do? And the Sun above said that he had watched over men and all creatures and all would obtain their deserts. And he drew ever closer to Earth, became ever dearer to her; the more she took of his sunlight, the more she loved him, grew like him, felt closer to him; the more did sunlight enter into her being and fill her with itself until she became golden with sunlight; golden her fields, wrapped and robed in gold; golden her trees which now stood glorious in autumn sunlight. Without stint Earth spent herself, gave all her riches, all of herself to her creatures, and they harvested her resources, stored up her bounty against the coming winter. From none did she withhold. Golden she grew, golden in her heart, for the Sun himself came down and they became one; the Sun entered and shone through her, and glorified her being; so that she herself became harvest for all creatures.

Like His Earth, God too gives of Himself in this fashion, which is the pattern of His universe, a universe in which all things are created for self-giving. And in men's hearts they too can bring their God to harvest home.